W9-ADV-971

Barry M. Kroll

TEACHING
Hearts and Minds

College Students
Reflect on the
Vietnam War
in Literature

Southern Illinois
University Press

Carbondale and
Edwardsville

Printed in the
United States of America

Design and production
by Natalia Nadraga

95 94 93 92   4 3 2 1

Library of Congress Cataloging-in-Publication Data

Kroll, Barry M., 1946–
    Teaching hearts and minds: college students reflect on the
Vietnam War in literature / Barry M. Kroll.
        p. cm.
    Includes bibliographical references and index.
    1. American literature—20th century—Study and teaching (Higher)
2. Vietnamese Conflict, 1961–1975—Literature and the conflict—
Study and teaching (Higher) 3. Vietnamese Conflict, 1961–1975—
Public opinion—United States. 4. War stories, American—Study and
teaching (Higher) 5. War poetry, American—Study and teaching
(Higher) 6. College students—United States—Attitudes. I. Title.
PS228.V5K7 1992
810.9'358—dc20   91-2868
    ISBN 0-8093-1748-6   CIP

The paper used in this publication
meets the minimum requirements
of American National Standard for
Information Sciences —Permanence
of Paper for Printed Library Materials,
ANSI Z39.48-1984. ∞

Contents

Those of us who did make
it have an obligation
to build again,
to teach others what we
know, and to try, with
what's left of our lives,
to find a goodness
and meaning to this life.

—Chris Taylor's
final reflections
in Oliver Stone's
Platoon

Preface

This book has its roots in an English course that I began teaching to undergraduates about five years ago, a course that uses the literature of the Vietnam War to stimulate reflection on personal, literary, epistemological, and moral issues. In fall 1986 and again in fall 1989, I taught the course to classes of about 140 college freshmen; in spring 1986 and spring 1988, I taught it to smaller groups of upperclassmen. Those students—more than three hundred, altogether—are the focus for this book, and their words occupy a prominent place in the text that follows.

Although this is a book about teaching and learning, it is not, strictly speaking, a pedagogical work, since my aim has not been to discuss how to teach a course on the war and its literature. Nor is it primarily a theoretical book. That is not to say that pedagogical and theoretical issues were unimportant to my project or that they will be ignored in the following pages. In fact, I will have some things to say about the kinds of "teaching practices" that foster reflective thinking, and I will argue that those practices are embedded in a broadly conceived "pragmatist" orientation to inquiry. But readers who are looking either for explicit pedagogical advice or for detailed theoretical argument will be disappointed. Instead, they will find a book based on my investigations of college students' processes of reflective inquiry.

In each of the four central chapters of the book, I report what I learned about a different domain of inquiry. In the first of these chapters, I consider students' attempts to build emotional or personal bridges to the war—their efforts to engage in what I will call "connected inquiry" into the nature of the Vietnam experience. In the chapter entitled "Literary Inquiry," I explore students' strategies for assessing different modes of writing about the war, especially their responses to books that violated their expectations about combat narratives. In the next chapter, "Critical Inquiry," I examine students' efforts to decide what really happened in the past, particularly when they were faced with competing versions of an event. And in the chapter "Ethical Inquiry," I focus on students' strategies for deciding what is right and wrong in war, a context where killing is legitimate and destruction the norm.

I should point out that, in both conception and execution, my project was a teacher's inquiry, characterized by my proximity to the course and my involvement with the students. If that involvement sacrificed some measure of objectivity, it also provided a vantage point from which to observe—with some acuity and accuracy, I believe—what was happening in my students' hearts and minds as they inquired into some of the issues raised by the Vietnam War and its literature. But I admit that my investigations were never marked by the degree of scientific control or detached impartiality that is sometimes equated with rigorous and objective research. My aims were more exploratory, my methods more informal and interpretive, than the word "research" usually suggests in educational circles.

If my project was not educational research, then what kind of investigation was it? Some might consider it a variety of field work or a type of ethnographic inquiry. But I tend to think of it as a close relative of "investigative journalism." I have in mind the journalism practiced by those reporters who strive to immerse themselves so thoroughly in situations that they can write their stories from the inside, and yet who commit themselves to fulfilling the journalist's contract to tell the truth. Like those journalists, I have tried to embrace both "subjectivity" and "objectivity," being true to what I saw happening in my classroom and faithful to what my students said about their experiences in the course.

Preface

In addition to bearing the marks of an investigative aim, this book has also been shaped by a secondary impulse: to demonstrate some of the possibilities of undergraduate education, exploring what can happen when students are engaged by a topic and encouraged to inquire into it. Thus there is a strand in the book that is frankly celebratory: I want to tell readers how exciting this course was for both teacher and students. Because I focus on my successes, however, there is a very real danger of sounding self-congratulatory. The danger is most acute in the final chapter, where I try to assess the significance of the Vietnam course. My strategy has been to allow the students to speak for themselves, using *their* words—excerpts from interviews, journals, and written exercises—to describe their responses to assignments and activities. The students said some rather remarkable things about the importance of the class, and I feel obliged to include those comments, even at the risk of being thought proud or pompous.

I need at the outset to clarify some things about the excerpts that will play such an important role throughout this book. My method of identifying the writers of these passages will be to use pseudonyms for a small number of students whose work I discuss at length, but for others to use a code to indicate each writer's gender (M or F), college class (FR, SO, JR, SR), and the semester and year the student was enrolled in my course. Both of the small courses for upperclassmen were offered in spring semesters (designated by an S): one in 1986 (S86) the other in 1988 (S88). The lecture courses for freshmen were both offered in fall (F) semesters, one in 1986 (F86) and the other in 1989 (F89). Thus, whenever I include an excerpt from a student I will identify his or her gender, college class, and course, placing that information in brackets following the quotation. (The one exception is chapter 6, where these notations are unnecessary and potentially confusing.) For example, the notation [F/FR/F86] indicates that the student was a female freshman who took my lecture class in fall 1986. I hope this code will be an unobtrusive way to provide

Preface

information that some readers will find relevant to my analyses of students' responses and reflections.

During five years of investigating and writing, I have incurred a number of debts to individuals who challenged my thinking and encouraged my work. During an early phase of the project, I had the good fortune to be part of a group called the Multidisciplinary Seminar on the Experience of War, a group funded by the Dean of Faculties at Indiana University. In that seminar, I had an opportunity to test my emerging ideas with colleagues who shared my interests but brought diverse perspectives to bear on them: D'Ann Campbell (history), Larry Davidson (business economics), John Lovell (political science), and Richard Miller (religious studies). Later, I was able to discuss parts of my project in another interdisciplinary forum, the working group on Culture and Conflict, sponsored by Indiana University's Center for Global Change and World Peace.

When I came to the stage of writing the first full draft of the manuscript, I had the wholehearted support of my department chair, Mary Burgan, who not only arranged for me to teach the Vietnam course at important times but also supported my application for a sabbatical leave at a point that was critical for my work. Because of that leave during spring 1989, I was able to complete a draft of the book by early summer, and I proceeded to inflict it on a half dozen colleagues and friends, all of whom gave unselfishly of their time to read and comment on the manuscript. I am grateful for the detailed and supportive responses of four colleagues in the English Department at Indiana University—William Burgan, Kathryn Flannery, Donald Gray, and Eugene Kintgen—as well as for helpful comments from David Smith, director of Indiana's Poynter Center for the Study of Ethics and American Institutions. Anne Ruggles Gere, a longtime friend from the University of Michigan, also responded to the manuscript. And I profited greatly from the advice of the graduate students who helped me teach the freshman courses, especially Allison Berg, Anne Bratach, Dulce Cruz, Kathy Hutnik,

Preface

Steve Wilhoit, and Lori Williams.

Armed with so many responses to the first full draft, I worked throughout 1989 and 1990 to revise the manuscript, adding material I collected when I taught the course in fall 1989 and completing a substantially rewritten draft by early summer 1990. Don Gray, who had commented so fully and helpfully on the first draft, scrutinized the new version. And my good friend John C. Schafer, from Humboldt State University, read this revised draft and gave me the kinds of comments that only a real Vietnam scholar—and one who has also taught the literature of the war—could provide. The revised manuscript also went to Southern Illinois University Press, where Kenney Withers received it with considerable enthusiasm and encouragement. His faith in my project was essential in the final stages. But my greatest debt of gratitude is to my wife, Diana Lambdin Kroll, who throughout the entire project provided the emotional and intellectual support without which this inquiry would not have been possible.

As this project draws to an end, I am struck by the parallels between my activities during the last five years and the activities I tried to arrange for the students in my courses. All of us, students and teacher alike, struggled to learn what it meant to be reflective inquirers: the students inquiring into the war and its literature, their teacher exploring what was happening in their hearts and minds. I learned as much about inquiry as they did, and there were numerous occasions when the students taught their professor as much as he taught them. Therefore, my final word of thanks goes to the undergraduates in my classes on the literature of the Vietnam War, so many of whom committed themselves wholeheartedly to the course. Without them, there would have been no book to write.

TEACHING
Hearts and Minds

1 Reading, Writing, and . . . Vietnam?

"Literature of the Vietnam War" said the Indiana University Bulletin. Hmm, I thought. Here I am, some scared little freshman at orientation, and this advisor wants to put me in a Vietnam literature class. His only basis for doing this is the fact that I had mentioned that I was remotely interested in a "different" English class. I was interested in a class where I would not have to read through one more act of "Hamlet," "Ghosts," or "Macbeth." I was also interested in history, especially Vietnam, so I decided to take the class. It has probably been the best decision of my life. [F/FR/F86]

Fifteen years after I returned from a tour of duty in Vietnam, I found myself preparing to teach a course on the literature of the Vietnam War—a task I could not have imagined in July 1970, when the wheels of my "freedom bird" left the runway at Tan Son Nhut air base, taking me back to "the world." Although I served with a support unit rather than a combat outfit, I still saw enough during 1969 and 1970 to make me want to put the war and the military behind me. Like many other soldiers, I returned from Vietnam eager to get on with my life. I went to graduate school, earned a Ph.D., and then began a career as a college teacher—an English professor, specializing in rhetoric and composition. I had little interest in the war or its literature.

But a decade later, the war was a topic of conversation again. By the mid-1980s, Vietnam veterans had been "welcomed home," their fallen comrades memorialized. Hollywood began to release a string of films—POW movies, revenge sagas, combat films—generating renewed interest in the war, if not always new insight. And, in increasing numbers, serious writers began to deal with the war in memoirs, novels, and books of poetry.[1] As this flow of books grew from a trickle to a torrent, I became curious about how the war was being represented and remembered. Tentatively, then avidly, I began to explore this burgeoning literature. And the more I read, the more clearly I could imagine myself teaching a course that focused on those provocative books.

Still, I had misgivings. For undergraduates in the mid-1980s, Vietnam was "history," an event as remote as the Korean Conflict or the war against Japan. Would my college students care about a conflict that, from their perspective, was a long-ago war in a far-away place? Could I expect the Vietnam literature, so salient and significant for me, to interest them? Was I imposing my own fascination with the war on a different generation?

Perhaps. But I began to suspect that my students would be engaged by the books I was reading. For one thing, many of those books were about men and women in their late teens or early twenties—exactly the age of my college students. Also, I discovered that undergraduates were intrigued by Vietnam, eager to know more about a war that was largely a mystery to them. But most important of all, I sensed that college students wanted to wrestle with the complex and provocative issues that the literature of the Vietnam War raises. In fact, the best books about the war are not just about Vietnam, nor are they only about war and peace. Rather, those books address such fundamental human issues as truth and falsehood, certainty and skepticism, faith and doubt, right and wrong, good and evil, illusion and

2

reality. A course that focused on the best of the war literature could be—would almost *have* to be—about more than Vietnam.

Thus it was my discovery of a literature replete with epistemological and ethical issues—more than my own personal concerns and connections with the war—that persuaded me to teach a course about the Vietnam War in literature.[2] Those issues were important because I did not want to teach a traditional course in literary appreciation and analysis. Rather, my sights were set on the kind of course that would engage students' emotional and intellectual resources, a course that would teach them to use their "hearts and minds" (to appropriate an infamous slogan from the war).[3]

Between January 1986 and December 1989, I taught the course four times: twice to relatively small groups of upperclassmen and twice to large classes of freshmen.[4] The students in those classes were quite representative of the undergraduates that I have taught at public universities in the Midwest: they hailed from farms and cities, from the rural hill country as well as the northern industrial belt. But nearly all of them were white and middle class, and they shared, for the most part, traditional American values and aspirations. They also shared a startling lack of knowledge about the Vietnam War. As one freshman put it: "I was basically clueless concerning all aspects of the war" [F/FR/F86].

I should not have been surprised by how little they knew about the war. The oldest students in the first class I taught were still in elementary school when American troops left Vietnam. Those students had, at best, vague memories of the war. One wrote that he was "intrigued by this thing I barely remember watching on TV years ago" [M/SR/S86]. For the youngest students in the class I taught in 1989, the war was more legend than reality: born during the final years of American involvement in Vietnam, they had no memory and very little knowledge of that period. And with few exceptions, students told me that Vietnam was almost totally ignored in their high-school history courses.[5]

3

Since our history classes never got far enough to cover the Vietnam War, I never thought about it. For a while, I confused the Vietnam and Korean Wars. They both occurred in the Far East, they both had a problem with northern communists trying to invade the south, and in both situations America intervened. [F/FR/F89]

My course was not about the history and politics of America's sad involvement in Indochina: if students hadn't learned about the war in their history courses, I couldn't hope to remedy that situation in an English class, especially one that purported to teach reading, writing, and critical thinking. The best I could do was to provide an overview of the conflict and then make certain that students knew, from the outset, that my course would focus on literary and philosophical issues. If students wanted to consider additional questions, I recommended courses in the history and political science departments, where the causes and consequences of the war were examined in depth. In my course, however, we would focus on literature: a series of books about the Vietnam War, written from the perspective of the American men and women who fought there.

I chose the most provocative readings I could find, books that promised to engage students' emotional and intellectual resources, to captivate their hearts and minds. Although I changed some of the texts each semester, the major units and core readings stayed the same: I always began with traditional memoirs and proceeded to more complex and innovative kinds of writing, considering with each new mode problems of method and aim, style and trustworthiness. Let me sketch out the sequence of units and major texts. (Texts and the semesters I used them are listed in appendix C.)

In the first unit, students read selections from Al Santoli's collection of "oral histories," *Everything We Had*. The short, powerful recollections in this book grabbed students' attention: here were men and women talking frankly about experiences that most students found shocking and troubling. I encouraged students to compare the experiences of soldiers who had different kinds of assignments, or who were stationed in different parts of the country, or who served during different periods of the war.[6] With each new account, students became more cognizant of the variety and complexity of "the" Vietnam experience. As one student put it, the readings in Santoli "shattered the illusion that every soldier's experience was the same" [M/SR/S86]. Stereotypes and simple generalizations gave way to a richer and more complicated conception of what the war was like for the people who fought in it.

During the second unit, students read selections from two book-length memoirs, one by a man (Philip Caputo's *Rumor of War*) and one by a woman (Lynda Van Devanter's *Home Before Morning*). To encourage comparative analysis, I arranged the assignments so that students read related parts of the memoirs together. Thus the first readings focused on the writers' backgrounds and reasons for joining the military. Both authors talk about a patriotism inspired by John F. Kennedy's challenge to "ask what you can do for your country." But Caputo joined the Marines as much from a thirst for adventure and excitement as from political idealism: attracted by a Marine recruiting poster and tales of adventure, he decided to enlist. Conversely, Van Devanter joined the military because of a sense of care and responsibility for others who were sacrificing themselves in a noble cause. Subsequent readings focused on the two authors' war experiences. Caputo arrived in Vietnam with the first wave of Marines in March 1965, and although his mission was at first strictly defensive, his brigade soon adopted a strategy of "aggressive defense," beginning long-range patrols and search-and-destroy operations. Van Devanter arrived in Vietnam in June 1969. She was assigned to the 71st Evacuation Hospital at Pleiku and thrown quickly into duty in the operating room, where she confronted a seemingly endless stream of blasted and broken bodies—the horrors of pain, disfigurement, and death. Caputo worked as hard as he could to kill; Van Devanter worked

5

tirelessly to heal. Nevertheless, both writers tell essentially the same tale: the story of war as a passage from innocence to experience, from naiveté and idealism to disillusionment and cynicism.

The move into the third unit involved a transition from reading personal accounts to examining reports and analyses of a specific event: the Vietnamese Communists' twenty-five day occupation of the city of Hué during late January and February 1968 (part of the Tet Offensive, a Viet Cong attack against the major cities in South Vietnam). By the time U.S. and South Vietnamese units recaptured Hué, much of this beautiful and historic city lay in ruins, and a large number of its citizens—perhaps three thousand or more—were missing or dead. According to one view, Communist forces systematically massacred many of these South Vietnamese civilians. But according to a second view, official reports of a planned massacre were actually an elaborate "myth," concocted to conceal the fact that many of the dead and missing civilians could be attributed to the ruthlessness of the U.S. counterattack against Hué. Students were given the task of examining these conflicting claims and writing a paper in which they presented the best case they could for what really happened in Hué during Tet 1968.

To this point in the course, students had read personal narratives and straightforward reports and analyses of events, types of writing that they found familiar and accessible. However, in the fourth unit, when they read Michael Herr's *Dispatches*, students encountered a text that was neither a simple narrative, nor a chronological account, nor a conventional analysis. By juxtaposing *Dispatches* with more traditional reporting on the Tet Offensive, students would, I hoped, be able to assess Herr's claims about the limits of conventional reporting. And they would better appreciate Herr's efforts to craft a new, "literary" journalism, a kind of reporting that makes generous use of stories, dialogue, striking images, rich descriptions of people and places, and above all the language of the men who fought the war.

Reading, Writing, and . . . Vietnam?

In one version of the course, I followed the unit on literary journalism with Yusef Komunyakaa's book of poems, *Dien Cai Dau*. The connection with *Dispatches* was straightforward: Herr's attention to language and image is clearly "poetic," a point that students did not miss. But in other versions of the course I moved from literary journalism to war fiction. This transition, too, was relatively easy: Herr's writing falls between the traditional categories of factual reporting and fictional writing—the content is journalistic, the techniques novelistic. Thus our discussion of Herr's writing techniques led naturally to a unit on fiction as a mode of writing about the war.

Sometimes I asked students to read two novels, sometimes only one. When I used two novels, I began with James Webb's *Fields of Fire*. Webb's aim is to portray, as accurately as possible, the multiple dimensions of the war, especially as it was experienced by men in the infantry. To do so, he adopts many of the conventional techniques of fiction in the "representational realist" mode: he uses a third-person omniscient narrator; tells the story chronologically (except for a brief prologue and occasional character sketches); portrays his characters by recounting their actions, thoughts, and conversations; and places those characters in a series of situations that represent typical experiences and dilemmas for the combat soldier in Vietnam.

The other novel, Tim O'Brien's *Going After Cacciato*, is a striking contrast to Webb's book. O'Brien tells the implausible story of Cacciato, an infantryman who grows tired of the war and runs away to the west, toward civilization. His squad, including the central character, Pfc Paul Berlin, pursues him—out of Vietnam, through Indochina, Southeast Asia, Iran, and Greece, and finally across Europe to their destination: Paris. About half the chapters in the book tell this story as it unfolds, using techniques appropriate for a realistic narrative but with fantastic and magical episodes. Interspersed with these chapters about the journey, however, are chapters that relate details from Paul Berlin's six months of duty in Vietnam. We get snatches of Berlin's memories

7

as he struggles to recall the men in his squad: who they were (ordinary men) and how they died (not heroically). Although most students learned to appreciate this novel, they also found it to be one of the most complex and demanding assignments in the course.

In the sixth and final unit, students considered some of the "legacies" of the war, usually by reading another memoir. In one version of the course, students read Ron Kovic's *Born on the Fourth of July*, a disturbing tale of a young Marine's struggle to cope with his wounds (he comes home paralyzed from the waist down), his guilt (he was involved in the unintentional killing of some children and a fellow soldier), and a deep rage that transformed a patriotic young man into an activist in the anti-war movement. Another time, I concluded the course with *Brothers in Arms*, William Broyles's account of his return to Vietnam to meet his old enemies, as well as a thoughtful reflection on the nature and meaning of the war.

When I taught the course for the first time in spring semester 1986, I was surprised by the intensity of students' reactions to these books, the depth of their involvement in the course. But it was an intense experience for me as well. In fact, teaching that first class was so exhilarating, its effects on students so palpable, that I spent the next four years teaching the course to other groups of undergraduates and trying to understand what happened when they confronted the issues that the war and its literature raised for them.

Because I wanted to explore what was going on in my students' heads and hearts as they read the Vietnam literature, I had to find ways to get inside their thoughts and feelings. I tried different approaches. Sometimes I talked with them in lengthy interviews. Sometimes I designed projects to elicit their reflections on key issues. But the most useful method I found was simply to ask students to keep a journal of their reactions and moments of insight. Therefore, as one of the course requirements, students had to make regular, detailed, and thoughtful entries in their journals each week.[7] In nearly every case, the journals provided a remarkably clear window into students' responses and reflections as they read the literature of the Vietnam War.

At the end of each semester, I photocopied (with students' permission) a selection of journals, choosing those that contained a range of interesting, but also representative, comments on the texts and issues that were most central to the course. Altogether, I copied seventy journals from the four courses I taught between 1986 and 1989.[8] Throughout this book, I make generous use of excerpts from those journals, using them not only to document my observations but also to render the students' responses in their own words.

However, strings of excerpts—even when they are interesting—inevitably interrupt the exposition and soon become repetitious. In the interest of readability, therefore, I've used only one or two excerpts to illustrate what students said on a particular topic, and I've attempted to keep those quotations brief.[9] Obviously, a couple of excerpts cannot represent everything students said, and one or two quotations do not suggest how often certain kinds of statements appeared in the journals. Therefore, I use terms such as "many," "some," or "a few" to indicate—in an approximate but, I trust, useful way—something about the frequency with which I saw various responses in the students' journals.

The short excerpts have another limitation: they do not provide a picture of what it meant for a student to wrestle with an issue over a period of days or weeks, or indeed what the course experience as a whole was like for a particular individual. To give a better sense of that experience, I will be tracing the responses of one student (a freshman named Karen) through each chapter, briefly in the early chapters, but at some length in later ones.

By exploring students' responses and reflections, I hoped to understand their feelings and thoughts as they read the literature of the war and wrestled with the issues that those books raise for their readers. But what I learned from those explorations was relevant for my teaching as well, because it enabled me to tailor my lectures, discussion questions, and written comments to students' needs and concerns. I found myself shuttling back and forth between two roles, striving to be both "instructor" and "investigator," activities that turned out to be quite compatible, in fact, because in both roles I was oriented to reflective inquiry.[10]

As a teacher, I was attracted to the concept of inquiry because, after a decade of college teaching, I was convinced that the way to foster genuine thinking was by focusing on questions rather than answers, on problems rather than solutions. In my courses, therefore, I wanted students to explore, probe, query, investigate—in short, to inquire. I had no "content" that I wanted to pour into students' heads, no facts for them to memorize, no exams on which they were expected to display their knowledge. Of course students would need to learn something about the context for the Vietnam War and some basic facts about how it was fought. My goal was not, however, to get students to *acquire* a body of information about the war; rather, I wanted them to *inquire* into the issues raised by literature of the Vietnam experience.

Moreover, I wanted students' inquiries to be "reflective": grounded not in dogma, prejudice, or impulse, but based instead on analysis—on interrogative, comparative, and evaluative thinking. Thus my work as a teacher was rooted in a broadly conceived "pragmatist" orientation to pedagogy. John Dewey's book *How We Think* was a central influence, and his concept of "reflective inquiry" gave focus to my project and direction to my teaching.[11] In Dewey's view, reflective thinkers suspend judgment while they inquire more deeply into alternatives: they "weigh, ponder, deliberate" (175), seeking to "establish belief upon a firm basis of evidence and rationality" (118). Or as Dewey defines it in a key passage, reflective thought involves "active, persistent, and careful consideration of any belief or supposed form of knowledge in the light of the grounds that support it and the further conclusions to which it tends" (118).

But there is more: reflective thinking also involves the passions that drive committed inquiry. As Dewey says so emphatically:

> Human beings are not normally divided into two parts, the one emotional, the other coldly intellectual. . . . Unless there is a fusion of the intellectual and the emotional. . . . problems and questions, which are the only true instigators of reflective activity, will be more or less externally imposed and only half-heartedly felt and dealt with. (341)

Because inquiry is an affair of the heart as well as the mind, students must feel connected to a topic if they are going to inquire deeply and honestly into it. One of my aims, therefore, was to make emotional response and personal connection an integral part of the course. In sum, I wanted to promote the kind of committed, reflective thinking that Dewey talks about so cogently.

Because I was determined to foster *reflective* thinking, I tried to devise activities and assignments that would encourage students to review their ideas and examine their views. To "reflect" means to turn back on one's thoughts. As Dewey says, reflection "consists in turning a subject over in the mind and giving it serious and consecutive consideration" (113). How could I foster that kind of reflective consideration? The best method I found was regular writing in the journal. I said earlier that the journal provided a window into students' responses and reflections, but journal writing also gave my students the means for some serious inquiries into significant issues.

Students used the journal mainly as a response log, recording their thoughts and feelings as they read the assignments or pondered issues that the course raised for them.[12]

By writing in the journal, I found myself having to deal with issues that . . . I probably would not have dealt with otherwise.

Having to write my responses down forced me to really think about many tough issues that I did not know if I wanted to face. [F/FR/F86]

But the journal also encouraged students to review their ideas. Occasionally, review and revision occurred even while students were writing their entries, a process that is clear in the following excerpt.

The fact is, *and I'm just realizing this as I write*, that I don't think of our soldiers' killing as actual killing. I think of their killing as something that was necessary and understandable. (emphasis added) [F/FR/F86]

More typically, students realized, when they reread their entries, that there were contradictions or changes in their views.

God, I was just reading over my journal. I *completely* contradicted myself in a matter of five pages. This is weird. [F/FR/F86]

To foster this important process of review, at key points in the semester I asked students to look back through their entries and write about what they found. Usually I asked for a review at midterm, and I always made the final assignment a "retrospective reflection," a short paper based on a review of the journal. Because they had a written, chronological record of their thoughts and feelings, students could compare their ideas and modes of inquiry at the end of the course with earlier manifestations of their thinking. Sometimes they were surprised by what they saw:

I just finished typing my final reflection paper. It was truly amazing to go back and read my first entry. It's like a calculus student going back to review the addition of whole numbers! [M/FR/F89]

When they read through their completed journals, students recognized how much they had learned and how far they had come in their thinking.

Reading, Writing, and . . . Vietnam?

As I sit reading my journal, I feel a little embarrassed at some of my earlier passages. The embarrassment doesn't come so much from my earlier convictions on the war, though I must admit they did evolve into a much deeper understanding of what actually went on. What makes me laugh, grimace, and roll my eyes is the way I sound: righteous and overly confident that I knew pretty much what happened, thinking in the far corners of my mind, "Shit, I just hope we don't go over a bunch of stuff I already know." Hah. I was shocked at all there was that I'd never even heard of or previously considered. [M/SR/S88]

Those tattered journals, most of them about fifty pages long, were important to students. As one freshman said at the end of the semester:

I don't have some stupid notebook full of someone else's words from lectures. I have my own notebook full of my words, which is really important to me. [F/FR/F89]

And in many cases, the journals were records of a significant personal journey.

As a requirement for this class, I needed a cardboard binder for my journal. Thus, at the beginning of the year I purchased such a binder at the bookstore. I remember I chose a crisp, new, red folder, being careful it had the proper tabs for loose-leaf notebook paper; inside, there was nothing else. Sitting on my desk now . . . my journal is dirty and worn, and when I hold it I notice how thick and heavy it's become. Completed, my journal is full of my entries and it is worth much more than the day I bought it. Since that first day, my journal has traveled far, and . . . so have I. [F/FR/F86]

Although the informal, unstructured writing seemed to have a special power to elicit reflection, it was not the only activity that encouraged thoughtful deliberation. Students also wrote in response to assignments and special problems. In every course, I assigned between four and six analytical essays. Those essays often grew out of journal entries, but they called for a different kind of writing: papers in which students were expected to de-

13

fend a comparative and evaluative judgment about books, authors, or issues.

I also asked students to write about a pair of "problems" or "dilemmas" at both the beginning and end of the course. In one dilemma, a soldier has to decide whether to shoot a peasant woman who might be a threat to his comrades; students were asked what the soldier should do. The other problem posed a situation in which there were two different accounts of the same battle; students were asked if either account was more likely to be true. I assigned these problems during the first week of class, collected the responses, and then, at the end of the course, asked students to write about the same situations again. A few days later, I returned both responses and distributed a worksheet on which to compare them. Students found this final step to be a provocative exercise, stimulating reflection on the ways in which their beliefs and modes of justification had either shifted or remained stable. I will have quite a bit to say about the responses to these two problems in subsequent chapters.

In addition to journal writing, projects, and papers, students had many opportunities to talk with one another about their responses and reflections. Although discussion was a major component of my small classes, even in the large lecture courses students met twice a week in discussion sections (twenty-five participants), conducted by a graduate-student assistant or, in some cases, by me. I had most success when I broke the small sections into even smaller groups, each with only four or five members. These small groups met about once every two weeks, at a time outside of the regular class period. (I canceled one of the discussion meetings as compensation.) The intimacy and informality of these smaller groups promoted more interaction among students, encouraging even the shy and quiet ones to express their views publicly. I remember one student in particular who never spoke in the larger group, a bright student whom I had encouraged, without much success, to try to overcome her shyness. After the first of the small-group meetings she wrote in her journal:

I really enjoyed the small group meeting we had on Friday. I actually spoke up! Did I shock you? It was painless. I even liked it! A breakthrough, maybe? [F/JR/S86]

Another time, a group of students organized—on their own initiative and without my knowledge—a meeting before class in one of the student lounges. The first I heard about this group was in a paper that one of the participants submitted near the end of the semester.

Sort of by accident a number of the class members began assembling downstairs in the Ballantine Commons before class began. The interesting thing about these meetings was that they began to take the shape of a forum where different people would represent different points of view. . . . The topics of these discussions covered a wide array of issues. We discussed the topics we were covering in class, of course, but I think the most significant characteristic of those forums was that the class topics opened the door to other issues. [M/SR/S88]

But it wasn't unusual for topics of discussion to escape the bounds of the classroom: many students wrote about conversations in the dorm and at home, with friends, parents, and other teachers. One student claimed that she talked incessantly about Vietnam with her roommates, even while they ate their dinner, "analyzing it over my stale peach cobbler and watered-down potatoes" [F/FR/F86]. A junior noted in her journal:

I've noticed that since I've begun this class I have about two or three conversations a day with people about things related to Vietnam. Before I know it, I'm roping people into questions like "What do you think about communism, the military, war, the draft, Vietnam?" I've talked to people I've known all my life, people I've met once, old people, young people, students, professors, and friends of friends. [F/JR/S86]

And one of the freshmen wrote about how eagerly she shared the course with her family, when she went home for Thanksgiving vacation.

This is the first time I've been home long enough to talk to my family about school and my classes. I finally had the chance today. On the way to my aunt's house for dinner, I told my brother all about my class and how excited I was about the paper I had just turned in. When I was confronted by all of the relatives, the question "How's school?" was endlessly repeated by everyone. No matter who I talked to, I think I mentioned something about this class and what I've learned. As we prepared for our dinner, we gave thanks for everything we were given. My thoughts were focused on Vietnam. "Thank you God, that I wasn't there." [F/FR/F89]

Whether they worked collectively or individually, in group discussions or in the privacy of their thoughts, within the classroom or without, students confronted issues and questions that called for heartfelt response and thoughtful reflection.

The first time I taught the course (spring semester 1986) I had a section with 25 students, mostly upperclassmen—an ideal setting for the kind of discussion-oriented class I was accustomed to teaching. In the fall semester, however, I was slated to teach the course under quite different conditions: a lecture class for 144 freshmen (the number of seats in the lecture hall). I was worried about how I would adapt the course for that new setting. I had no experience with lecturing, and frankly, I was skeptical about whether much could be achieved by talking at students for an hour. I was certain I would bore them and, even worse, convey the wrong message: suggesting that my course, like so many others in college, was designed to transmit information from an authority to a room full of empty minds. Traditional lectures would surely subvert my goals, encouraging a passivity that would be antithetical to active inquiry.

That fall, I went into the freshman course aware of the pitfalls of lecturing and prepared to try some alternatives for large-group instruction. But because I was new at it, I had to learn about the special opportunities afforded by a lecture hall filled to capacity. At the beginning of the semester, I did not suspect that a large audience could generate such a degree of emotional intensity. There were days when the energy crackled through the air, as though someone had wired all the students and plugged them into the main current. As one freshman wrote:

Someone asked me the other day, "How is your course on Vietnam?" . . . I gave a one-word answer, "Intense." There's no way anyone can ever *really* understand . . . unless they sit through it, take it all in—and this course is so much more than, well, English, it's—well, I'm still searching for a way to describe it, but until then I'll stick with "intense"! [F/FR/F86]

I worked hard to create that intensity, and at least part of it was due to the approaches I tried in the lecture class. Although I sometimes presented background information or talked about ways of reading difficult texts, I rarely lectured for the entire hour. Instead, I employed a variety of media, using music, slides, documentaries, and parts of movies to elucidate passages in our reading and to keep students engaged in the topics we were considering.

Music—the way to total expression. "Purple Haze" really clicked with me today. You could hear it throughout the room—*click!* Even though Professor Kroll only showed two pictures, I understood them, felt them so much more. [F/FR/F86]

There's a familiar adage that good teaching is "three-fourths theater": some days I was as much entertainer as educator. I let students taste C-rations, gave them a whiff of Vietnamese fish sauce (nuoc maum), brought in veterans to talk about their experiences, spoke frankly about my own involvement in the war. The students responded well to this variety. As one of them wrote at the end of the semester:

17

The way this course was presented was a bombardment of interesting techniques. The videos, music, films, pictures, etc. all covered the war from the visual/audio perspective instead of the same old hum-drum lectures that are so common in all my other classes. [M/SR/S88]

I tried to surprise students, to break the routine, to keep them engaged. One student wrote (with some exaggeration, surely):

It seems I have to brace myself for what might happen in class— God only knows, and I want to be prepared to handle anything. After I leave this class, I'm in a state of numbness. [F/FR/F89]

Sometimes I used the lectures to "model" the kind of engaged response and critical reflection that I hoped to foster: to that end, I showed my emotions, revealed my passions, demonstrated my processes of deliberation. As one of the freshmen commented after a lecture on *Dispatches*:

I can tell that Kroll loves *Dispatches*. Today in lecture I half expected him to jump up and down, shouting "I love this book. It's written so well. Look at what he does!" [F/FR/F86]

That kind of enthusiasm was important, I believed, simply to keep students motivated, to keep them working on hard questions and difficult issues. It was not an easy class.

On the first day of each semester, I warned students that the course would be demanding and perhaps disturbing: demanding because the reading and writing assignments would be heavy, the standards high; disturbing because they would be exposed to violence and brutality, as well as harsh and explicit language. The earthy language bothered some students more than others. As one woman wrote near the end of the course:

Considering that I come from a home where someone using the "f" word is subject to eviction, you may understand why reading some of the memoirs was a little unnerving. Let's just say that I'm glad my mother didn't take this course! [F/FR/F86]

But my warnings seemed mostly to confirm students' commitment to the course.

Day one really scared me! I'm not sure I can handle the work load or the reading material. Not that the reading would be too difficult for me to comprehend, but the stories described may be too graphic for my stomach. No matter how much work there is or how sick the stories may get, I think I'll stick with the class. [F/FR/F86]

However, on that first day there was no way that I could tell students exactly what was in store for them. I often thought about a scene from *Going After Cacciato* in which a group of men who have just arrived in Vietnam sit in some bleachers next to a beach, waiting for an orientation lecture. The instructor enters, sits facing the water, and stares silently at the sea for an hour. At the end of this period he stands, faces the new arrivals, and says, "All right. . . . That completes your first lecture on how to survive this shit. I hope you paid attention" (56).

Like that instructor, I was unable to prepare students for all that lay ahead in the course. Although I could warn them about the workload, the harsh language, and the violence, I could not explain that the most unsettling aspects of the course would have little to do with any of those things. Rather, the course was going to be disturbing because it would raise vexing issues, asking students to examine the bases for their beliefs about truth and falsehood, right and wrong. And because the course would touch those deeply rooted epistemological and moral orientations, I felt a special responsibility to empathize with students' struggles and demonstrate that I took their perplexities seriously. I wanted them to know that I cared not only about their intellectual and ethical development, but also about their personal well being. But I could not tell them that, either, on opening day.

When they received the syllabus on the first day of class, students knew that they were going to read a series of factual and fictional books about the Vietnam experience, and they expected, in an English course, to be asked to analyze and appraise the texts they were reading. Those expectations were largely accurate: literary judgments were going to be prominent. What students could not discern from the syllabus, however, was that four broad streams of reflective inquiry were going to run through the course. I call them *connected, literary, critical,* and *ethical* inquiry, and although they are not always distinct from one another, I discuss each of them in a separate chapter.

When I taught the course to that first group of undergraduates, I was aware that something unusual was happening: fervent cognition, energetic conception, intense reflection—proof that hearts and minds were working together. Students were thinking about serious issues, and not in the perfunctory ways that are all too common in college. Even that first semester, I realized that something significant was happening. But it took me several more years to understand it well enough to begin writing about it.

2 Connected Inquiry

Maybe that's been the best thing
about this course for me—making
me care by making me look at the
war through different sets of eyes,
not just thinking in terms of abstract
suffering but in terms of *real* suffering, of why people suffered and how
they suffered. [F/SR/S86]

The first readings in my course were personal narratives, accounts by American men and women who had served
in Vietnam. I began each semester by assigning some of the "oral
histories" in Al Santoli's collection, *Everything We Had*. Those
intense, emotionally charged stories always elicited powerful
responses: "Emotions come pouring out of me as I read," admitted one student [F/FR/F89]. Another freshman revealed the range
of feelings that were evoked in just the first week of the course.

I have been in the class for a week and have read the first seven
or eight stories. I have never read more powerful literature in
my life. Throughout many of the stories I wanted to cry, and
others I wanted to run and hide. [M/FR/F89]

From the outset, I told students that it was appropriate to be
affected by books about war, and I encouraged them to find
ways to build personal, emotional, and experiential bridges into
soldiers' stories. In short, I wanted to foster the kind of reading
that Karen—the freshman whose responses I will be considering
in each chapter—described in one of her journal entries:

When I read, I'm always trying to understand the authors, trying to understand their feelings, their actions, their words. I'm . . . looking for something with which I can really connect.

"Really connect": that phrase could have served as a motto for the course.

From the beginning of the semester, I encouraged students to use their journals to express and record their reactions, and many of them said that this informal writing enabled them to articulate and clarify their feelings.[1]

My personal feelings about the war are evident throughout the journal. It's made it easier to understand things when I've written them out. [F/FR/F86]

To get a grasp on our personal feelings . . . we were asked to keep a journal of ideas and problems we were feeling at the time. The journals allowed us to probe deeply into our own feelings and raise questions about the war. . . . I think that, for me, the journal was the single most important part of the course. [M/FR/F89]

But I wanted to do more than simply elicit emotive reactions. Therefore, I tried to nudge students' responses in two directions. A great deal of my effort went into encouraging students to *develop* their responses into thoughtful questions and reflective judgments, a process I will consider in three subsequent chapters. But I also tried to get them to *deepen* their responses, encouraging them to identify with soldiers' experiences, or to imagine what it would be like to be in combat, or to examine their personal reactions to killing. In this chapter, I want to explore students' efforts to engage in what I will call "connected" inquiry: a quest to understand the Vietnam experience by finding emotional and personal connections with it.[2]

Connected inquiry typically began with intense involvement in one of the personal narratives—often the oral histories, but almost invariably the memoirs. And the book that elicited the most potent responses, in every class I taught, was *Home Before*

Morning, Lynda Van Devanter's memoir about her service as an Army nurse. The following journal entries illustrate the extent of students' involvement in this book:

The first chapter . . . really blew me away. I cried. It just hit me really hard. [F/FR/F89]

What can I say except, "God—it was incredible!" I don't think I've ever been so affected by a piece of writing. [M/FR/F86]

I cried. . . . tears in my eyes. It was just the first chapter, too. [F/SO/F89]

A number of students commented on the extent to which they were drawn into Van Devanter's story, becoming so deeply involved in her experiences that they could not put the book down.

Home Before Morning just keeps getting better and better. I have never loved a book so much. I have recommended it to several friends. I just love it! I really have a hard time with reading, but this book is the first one I actually can't put down. I have laughed and I have cried through this whole book. My roommate thinks I'm nuts. [F/FR/F89]

Van Devanter's memoir was especially important to the women in my courses. The book appealed to them because of its personal tone and heartfelt perspective.

I am enjoying learning about a woman and her encounters in Vietnam. She seems to have a more personal view and takes my interest even more than the men we have read. Her writings really seemed to come from the heart. [F/FR/F86]

In addition, this book had a special quality of voice, one that women found particularly engaging. As one student put it:

I find that I really enjoy reading about . . . the war through the writing of women, who are usually the Vietnam nurses. I don't know if it's because I'm of the same sex or not. It seems to be less violent and harsh. Also, there's more caring in their voices coming through the pages. I have the strongest emotional feelings while I'm reading their stories. [F/FR/F86]

In addition to being sympathetic to authors (such as Van Devanter) who took a personal approach, women students also tended to be quite willing to express their emotional responses.[3] Some of the men, on the other hand, resisted connected inquiry. As one of the seniors wrote in an early journal entry:

My reservations center on the intense emotion of the subject. . . . I find it difficult to share the emotion of the subject matter and the somber tone of the class. I find it hard to believe that the stories I read for today were reality because I am so far removed from them. I think the most I can hope for is an intellectual understanding of the war. [M/SR/S88]

Nevertheless, a number of men seemed grateful for an opportunity to express their feelings.

I have never thought of myself as an open bundle of feelings. I have always been in control. Damn it, so many times [in this course] I have been ripped open and stirred up like I have never known. I have grown up with "don't cry or show outward emotion like that." Bullshit! So many times I have had to stop reading and walk away. [M/FR/F89]

I encouraged all of my students, both men and women, to express their feelings of connection with the people whose experiences they were reading about. And I tried to support those efforts by practicing what I preached: when I felt especially sad, angry, or excited, I let those emotions show—not in emotive outbursts, of course, but with an expression or tone of voice that communicated my concern and involvement. Some students were surprised that professors had any feelings. As Rosenblatt comments in *Literature as Exploration*: "The assumption of a mask of unemotional objectivity or impartial omniscience is one reason why teachers and college professors seem not quite human to their students" (130). By showing that I, too, had deeply felt responses to books and ideas, I hoped to build a human connection with my students.

As their involvement in the war and its literature intensified, a number of students reported that fears of war and death began to haunt them. Because they were reading so much about death and destruction, students could hardly escape contemplating their own mortality.

I've been thinking about death a lot lately. . . . I realize that it is closer than I ever really thought. . . . I think that it's making me realize that I'm not immortal myself. I will die too, and so will all my friends. It is just so scary to think about. It's like, I look at someone and think, what would I do if they weren't here? What I think I'm trying to get at is that these soldiers in Vietnam saw that every day. [F/FR/F89]

Fears of combat also began to surface, sometimes consciously, often in dreams.

Reading so much about this war is disturbing in some ways. Last night I had a nightmare that I had been drafted by the Marines and they wanted to take me away. [M/SR/S86]

I cannot believe how much and how deeply this class is affecting me. Last night I dreamed that a person (who was a friend of mine in the dream) got drafted to go to Vietnam. . . . It was so bizarre, because I never dream about stuff like that. I guess reading, watching, and writing about Vietnam is getting it into my head. [F/FR/F89]

Some students found themselves more intensely involved than they expected. As one student admitted near the end of the course: "I didn't realize how deep I got" [M/SR/F89]. And yet, while emotional involvement provided a basis for connected inquiry, that involvement by itself did not produce a deeper understanding of what the war was like for the men and women who served in Vietnam. To apprehend the experience of war, students also needed to use their empathetic imaginations: identifying with soldiers (and other participants) and imagining what combat felt like. As one student said quite emphatically: "I really need to be able to feel for the Americans, the South Vietnamese, even the enemy. If I can't do that, I might as well be taking a computer class" [F/FR/F86].

Beginning with the personal accounts in *Everything We Had*, students tried to identify with soldiers and to anticipate their own responses in similar circumstances.[4]

I've always wondered what it would be like to fight as these men did. After reading these stories, I don't think I want to find out. You ask yourself: Could I do that? Would I live or die? [M/SR/ S86]

And the two book-length memoirs usually provoked ever deeper expressions of empathy and identification. As I mentioned before, women felt a special affiliation with Lynda Van Devanter.

My first reaction to . . . Van Devanter's book was "she's just like me, just like any other girl, and very down to earth." I can relate to her. [F/FR/F86]

But a number of male students, too, identified with the style and attitude of Van Devanter's memoir.

Home Before Morning by Lynda Van Devanter is very interesting. Even though she is a woman, which is a big difference, I can still relate to her. I could see myself making some of the same decisions for almost the same reasons as she does. [M/FR/F89]

On the other hand, few women were drawn to *A Rumor of War*, so that it was primarily the men who identified with Philip Caputo, especially with his suburban, middle-class background and the feelings of boredom and alienation that drove him into the military.

I see Caputo's life much like mine. Parents who care, but the life of the suburbs is so boring it is unbelievable. . . . I tend to think I myself, like Caputo, would have signed up for the service after graduation from college. Just the thought of getting into a situation where there is conflict seems, even today, intriguing. [M/FR/F89]

Many students found that they could identify with at least one of the memoir writers, and most of them also discovered that they could build bridges from their own experiences to events in the lives of the soldiers they were reading about. Sometimes an incident in the dorm or on the athletic field sparked a connection.

I had an experience this weekend that may have captured the feeling of combat. Of course, I can't be sure, but I've noticed many of the same reactions in myself that the combat veterans have expressed. It happened during our Lacrosse game against Purdue. . . . I felt indestructable. I thought I was a badass. Also, I was very intent on inflicting pain. I mean, I was swinging my stick as hard as I could. I was trying to hit the Purdue guy between the pads. . . . If combat is anything like that, I can certainly understand how people become hooked. [M/SR/S86]

In other cases, students drew on painful experiences as a source of empathy and identification.

Yesterday I had my teeth pulled, and I was in a lot of pain. It made me think how bad the men who fought and got wounded must have felt. I know this is stupid, but I couldn't help but think about it. [F/FR/F86]

Several students remarked that traumatic experiences, such as automobile accidents, evoked feelings similar to those that soldiers talk about having during combat: fear, but also exhilaration.

I got a little too close to some of the issues of the course today when I got into a car accident. You may ask yourself what a car accident has to do with the Vietnam War, but I felt at least some of the physical symptoms of combat (the rush of adrenalin, shaky-yet-relieved feeling when it was over) when a woman pulled out onto the highway without seeing me, driving me off the road. [F/SR/S86]

27

Sometimes, identification involved active imagination, a concerted effort to picture oneself in a combat situation.

I wonder what it would be like to see myself and my friends turned into killing machines. . . . I imagine my whole fraternity put into a regiment. I wonder who would die, who would be crippled, who would be basket cases. I wonder who would love it, love the killing. I wonder if I would be willing to die for any of them; would any of them die for me? [M/JR/S86]

In other cases, students' imaginations were stimulated by a particular situation or setting.

I went to the Smokies for Spring Break, backpacking with fifty-pound packs for three days, and I was pretty worn out. I thought about the grunts carrying their heavy equipment on trails under triple canopy. As I was hiking, I thought about VC on all the ridges. How about if all of a sudden a sniper opened up on me and my friends. Whoa—I was scared in my intellectual exercise. [M/JR/S86]

And in a few cases, students sought out circumstances that would simulate aspects of the Vietnam experience.

I actually walked through the rain the other day specifically to attempt to feel the emotions that have been decribed to me in the readings. I thought of myself walking slowly in the wilderness, completely disgusted with my situation. All that I could consider was the dampness, cold, home. . . . I thought of myself reacting to gunfire and being thrown into a hostile situation. Life, death, responsibility, keep my friends alive, communicate without giving my position away. Where's my radio? Will I run out of ammo? How many VC are there anyway? [M/JR/S88]

One semester, a group of freshmen decided to enact a combat patrol, just to see what they could learn about the feelings that soldiers talk about it their accounts. Although the exercise was only a game, it evoked sensations of fear and confusion.

Connected Inquiry

Being put in a situation similar to those in Vietnam helped me realize how they felt when their lives were on the line. This mission really made me stop and think of what it would be like to know that at any minute you could be attacked. First of all, it amazed me how our class bonded together. None of us really knew each other, yet we all were trying to escape the same things—waterballoons. . . . Also I was so nervous and jumpy while we were on our mission. I was scared I would be hit at any minute. I now can understand what they went through. The only difference is I would be wet, they could be dead. I can't imagine being put through that every day. [F/FR/F89]

Most students believed that they could identify with the soldiers who fought in Vietnam, and many claimed that their reading, especially of personal narratives, brought them closer to the experience of war. But in a small number of cases, there was a disturbing consequence of this process of identification: the more students empathized with the plight of American soldiers, the less they sympathized with the Vietnamese. As one student noted:

As sad as it sounds . . . through these stories I have gained a negative, maybe even prejudiced feeling toward the Vietnamese people. I have read so many negative stories about them through American accounts. [F/SO/F89]

Sometimes the stories confirmed racial stereotypes and exacerbated students' prejudices. One student confronted these feelings with remarkable honesty.

An extremely disturbing thing happened to me today. . . . I was on my way to class when I passed several students (men) of Oriental descent. As I approached them, I got this feeling of resentment. When we passed, I shouldered one of the guys. . . . Anyway, I went to class and thought about what I had done. Not really any big deal, but in a way it was. I sometimes will look towards Orientals and get a feeling of hatred inside myself. Some of the readings have made me feel as if Orientals are untrustable, unloyal, and anti-American. [M/FR/F89]

29

To encourage students to examine their feelings about the Vietnamese, I tried to include opportunities to learn about Southeast Asians as people. I had the most success with *Brothers in Arms*, William Broyles's account of his return to Vietnam in 1984.[5] When he met his former enemies, Broyles discovered that they were very much like him, and he found that he "had more in common with my old enemies that with anyone except the men who had fought at my side" (263). After reading Broyles's book, some students began to revise their attitudes and responses, finding new ways of connecting both with the American soldiers and the Vietnamese.

Today . . . I really came to terms with the enemy. . . . I really realized that the Vietnamese—Viet Cong or not—were no different than the American soldiers. Their views, loyalties, and hearts were basically in the same place. At the beginning of the semester, I hated the Vietnamese. Now I feel sorry for them. I hate some of the things they did to us, but I also hate what we did to them. [F/FR/F89]

One of the most important things I learned is how to look at the war through the eyes of the Vietnamese. Before this class I was ignorant to . . . the fact that they were people, just like us. I dehumanized them like the Marines were taught. . . . I still feel for the American veterans, but I have a new found respect for the Vietnamese. . . . This realization about the Vietnamese was the most important thing I got out of this class. [M/FR/F89]

By involving themselves emotionally in the personal narratives, by identifying with soldiers' experiences, and also by imagining what it was like to be in a combat zone, quite a few students found ways to connect with the experiences they were reading about. These connections would always be approximations, of course. Students were well aware of the limits of their capacity to empathize and understand.

War is a different world—a world that you . . . cannot *fully* comprehend until, well, until you actually see one of your friends blown apart, lose a good friend, live on the edge of your life. [F/FR/F86]

I have no understanding of what it is like . . . to watch your buddies cry out in pain or have an arm blown off. . . . to walk a mile through elephant grass, to watch my feet disintegrate from jungle rot. I have no idea of the emotional and physical burden. [F/JR/S88]

For those students who tried to step into the soldiers' shoes, however, war became more familiar, less abstract. And many of them believed that they were getting closer to understanding what Vietnam had been like. As one of the seniors said: "This course has helped me to face . . . if only for a short time and in the abstract, some of the conflicts the people fighting in Vietnam had to face" [F/SR/S86].

Nevertheless, most students came to a point where they wanted to move beyond the readings: they wanted to talk with soldiers, making deeper connections by interacting with Vietnam veterans.

What I would enjoy more than anything, however, is to talk directly with a Vietnam veteran; to not only listen to him or her, but to see the facial expressions, hand movements, to see the story in his or her eyes—and to feel it. [F/FR/F89]

In the larger courses, I had to rely on men who were willing to speak to groups of students, sometimes to the entire class, sometimes to the smaller discussion sections. For example, when students were reading Van Devanter's account of her experiences in an evacuation hospital, I invited a local physician, who was a doctor at Khe Sanh during the seige of 1968, to speak to the large lecture class. His stories and slides confirmed the reality of what students had been reading about.

I'm really glad that I got to hear the doctor speak today. It was really hard for me to comprehend that he was *actually* there. Because I've read all these stories and I'm so caught up in *Home*

Before Morning . . . I forget that these stories are *real*. . . . I realized that this guy was *there*, in country, in the worst place at the worst time! All of a sudden, it just hit me. [F/FR/F89]

I also talked about my own experiences. Students were usually eager, even impatient, to hear my story.

Class was interesting today, but I really wish Dr. Kroll would just get personal. I want to know what it was like for him—his personal experience. [F/FR/F86]

But I felt that I had to handle carefully the time and manner in which I revealed that I had been in Vietnam. Usually I deferred this revelation until after the course was under way, avoiding a grand announcement the first day. I preferred to wait until after the students had read a number of personal accounts of the war, so that I could explain that my status as a veteran gave me *a* view of the war, not *the* view, and that my experience, like those we were reading about in the oral histories and memoirs, was simply another piece of a complex puzzle.

My story was not as dramatic as most of the personal accounts students read. I went to Vietnam as a twenty-three-year-old college graduate, an Army ROTC officer assigned to a noncombat branch (Transportation Corps), and I was based in a large and secure logistical complex—Long Binh. The most dangerous part of my tour was the time I spent as a convoy commander.[6] My line-haul truck battalion transported food and ammunition to most of the infantry units in the area west of Saigon (III Corps), primarily to bases near the Cambodian border. Attacks on our convoys were infrequent but sudden and vicious when they occurred, keeping us always on edge. Two months before I arrived in Vietnam, my unit was involved in a brutal ambush, one of the fiercest engagements in what military historian Shelby Stanton has called the "convoy battles of 1969" (289). I heard the story of that ambush one night shortly after I arrived at my truck company, as I drank a beer with the other platoon leaders. Their stories terrified me for weeks. I carried extra ammunition and sacks of grenades, certain that I would be cut off and overrun like the men on that ill-fated convoy. But I led a charmed life. I never endured a full-scale attack. Although I was shot at occasionally and rocketed now and then, there was never anything to shoot back at. I felt fully prepared to kill anyone who threatened me, but I never had to do it.

When I talked about my experiences, I tried to convey my own best sense of who I was in Vietnam: an average soldier trying to do a fairly routine job in a strange and frightening place. The students' reactions always interested me. Here is a perceptive one.

Today was the day that Dr. Kroll sat in on our discussion. I have always wondered why he was so interested in us learning about the Vietnam War and finding out the truth. It was very shocking to me to learn that he is a Vietnam veteran. It was as if when he told us about being in Vietnam everything clicked for me. I now see why he is determined to teach us about a very important period in history. . . . He has a purpose for teaching us, not like other profs. I also feel a personal touch, too. [F/FR/F89]

I also invited other veterans to talk with the discussion groups, trying to get a representative sample of experiences and attitudes: some combat veterans and some support troops, some professional soldiers and some draftees, some men who had dealt successfully with their experiences and some who had not. Sometimes these discussions were quite moving.

I tried to listen carefully to what Mr. _____ said, but also I watched his movements, face, etc. . . . At first he seemed very cold and harsh, "macho" described his mannerisms well. His posture, vocabulary, and tone of voice, also his movement were always bold, distinct, and to the point. . . . But after a while, it appeared that he was just very guarded—I think a lot of the "walls" he built in Vietnam are still there. . . . But I was touched (almost to tears) when he started to cry. [F/FR/F89]

Nevertheless, even the best of the group discussions, whether with me or other veterans, left students hungry for more intimate interactions: the chance "to sit down with a veteran and just talk one-on-one." [F/FR/F89]

Therefore, when I taught smaller sections of the course, I asked students to write a paper based on an interview with someone who had participated in the war. At first, some students were apprehensive about this assignment.

I approached my interview with a Vietnam veteran with some trepidation. I felt I would be intruding into this stranger's life, asking questions that were too personal. . . . I was fearful that I might trigger some sort of negative response in him. [M/JR/S86]

At first, I was a little apprehensive about the whole thing. Was this guy going to tell me horrible stories? Would he run off into a deep, dark mood? I can understand now why some people might be afraid to talk to Vietnam vets. [M/SR/S86]

When they conducted the interviews, however, the students were captivated by the veterans' accounts—caught up in the stories and deeply moved by the feelings they uncovered. And for some students, the interview experience was quite "intense."

I was in no way prepared for the things he had to say and the intensity with which he said them. . . . I found myself completely drawn into what he had to say and gripping the edge of the table until my knuckles were turning white. . . . I felt very numb for quite a while at the end of it. [M/SR/S88]

Both men I reported on were very emotional in telling me their story, and they touched me in a way that made me feel guilty and sad and sorry for them and what they went through. It became so real to me suddenly, and I didn't expect it. I thought I sort of understood some things because of our readings, but I don't think I did. Both men sounded so sad, so lonely or something. I could hear the pain in their voices. [F/JR/S88]

Interviews, even with strangers, provided potent connections to the war. But the most powerful interactions I heard about were those that took place within families. Some students wrote about how reticent their fathers and uncles had been to talk about their participation in the war.

My father was in the war. . . . He never talks about it. I knew that it must have been a painful experience for him, but now I can understand why. [F/FR/F86]

I went home this weekend and had a very unusual encounter with my uncle. My uncle was a Marine in Vietnam. . . . He's *never* talked about it to anyone—not his parents, brothers or sisters, or even his wife. [F/FR/F86]

My uncle served in Vietnam from 1969 to 1970 in Chu Lai. He has never talked about it, and I felt that if I took this course . . . I might understand more of what he was faced with over there. [F/FR/F89]

I saw several poignant cases in which students were eager, but at the same time reticent, to talk with relatives who had been soldiers. One of those students was Karen. On the first page of her journal, Karen foreshadowed the process that would provide her central connection with the war, stating quite simply: "My father was in the Vietnam War." About a week later, Karen mentioned that she had gone home over the weekend and talked with her mother "about the war and my father's participation in it. She asked me if Dad had really talked to me about his experiences because he never discussed it with her." Karen could recall only one war story. Then she commented in her journal:

I wonder now if he can't talk about some aspects or if he does have some horrible pictures in his mind. I don't even know, come to think of it, how he feels about the Vietnamese. . . . I think after reading all these accounts in Santoli's book, I realized how little I knew about how my father feels.

In mid-October, Karen went home to visit her mother again, and they "talked a little about Vietnam." In reflecting on this conversation, Karen recognized that her father is not the kind of person who would be disposed to reveal his feelings about Vietnam.

I would love to talk to him about some of the topics we've discussed, but I'm not sure how to approach him. As I said earlier, I do not know if his way of dealing with whatever it was he experienced is to suppress his feelings—to not want to talk about it. If that is so, I should respect it.

Finally, in early November, Karen got the chance she had been waiting for all semester.

This past weekend I talked to my father a little about Vietnam. I told him what we were doing in class, what we had read and seen and discussed. He seemed interested, yet distant.

They talked about some films Karen had seen and about the issue of atrocities committed by American soldiers: "He said he knew it happened, but he just never saw it." The conversation turned to the Americans' feelings about the Vietnamese, but Karen was reluctant to push too hard. "That is about all we talked about. I never want to ask too much because I still don't know how he'll react and I certainly want to respect his way of dealing with the war." Although he was reticient to talk about his experiences, Karen tried to interpret her father's facial expressions and mannerisms.

I have noticed that he is quite different when he talks about Vietnam than any other time he talks about different topics. He is much more serious, serene, almost cold. His face is very stone-like, expressionless, and he looks straight forward and yet seems to be looking at nothing—maybe seeing things inside his eyes, inside his mind, but he is not the type to express himself or reveal his feelings.

At the end of the course, when she summed up what she had learned, Karen made it clear how central the process of connected inquiry—especially the interactions with her father—had been for her.[7]

> I have also been able to talk with my father. I realize now that there may be more to him, more to his experience in the war, than I know or will ever know. And I can see when I talk to him that he has some very deep, very real feelings about Vietnam, and my respect for him has grown.

Although relatively few students had relatives who served in Vietnam, nearly all of them found ways to forge connections to the war, building a basis for understanding what the war was like and what it meant to the men and women who fought in it. In the process of connecting with soldiers' experiences, students were also led to look into their own hearts, probing their capacity for violence and examining their feelings about killing and dying. Once students began to imagine themselves standing in the soldiers' shoes, it was perhaps inevitable for them to reflect on what they would have done with a gun in their hands. Of those who asked themselves that fundamental question—"could I kill?"—some concluded that the answer was "no."

> I don't think I could ever kill someone in a war. I can't take away a human life. [F/SR/S88]

> I think if I had been sent to Vietnam, I would have ended up dead. I would have been the one eating a grenade on a split-second decision. I don't know why, I have just always had too much compassion for strangers. [M/SR/S88]

But a number of others found that the answer was "yes."

> I began to think and wonder if I could kill a human. I guess if it were in a time of war I could. I was shocked at my conclusion. . . . It scares me to think that I think I could kill! [F/FR/F86]

> I consider myself a pretty nonviolent person, but . . . I felt that I too could kill. [F/JR/S86]

37

I know I am capable of killing, even killing for fun if put in the right circumstances. [M/JR/S86]

I know I could have been taught to kill and to enjoy it. I can feel that part of myself without a doubt, and I believe women who don't see that part of themselves deny it. [F/JR/S86]

And some students acknowledged that war has its attractions—the allure of an incredibly intense experience.

I wish I could have lived through something like that—something that would drastically change my life. Maybe I just don't get it—how horrible war is. . . . I still see the adventure of it all! I can totally understand why men volunteered to go to Vietnam for this reason. I can *feel* it. I feel like I want to do something important or adventuresome. [F/FR/F89]

I really wish I could have been there. I don't really know how to justify that, and I don't really know what the attraction is. Yet, it is there and I feel it. . . . Nothing in my life has ever been contested. Nothing has ever asked me why I am here. . . . Maybe in a situation as dangerous as those were, and the possibility of injury is all around, surviving is kind of like God breathing life into you all over again. Maybe that is the attraction. [M/SR/S86]

Could I enjoy this experience? War is hell, I always thought. But God, at times it has to be such a rush. . . . There's got to be something of a thrill knowing that you have some power. God for a day. I can blast, waste, wax, deep-six you motherfucker, just by moving my index finger a fraction of an inch. [M/SR/S86]

It took courage to examine such deep feelings. As one student wrote:

Don't get me wrong. I could easily have written five pages on why war is a terrible experience to be avoided at all costs. That is relatively obvious and I think the attractions are more subtle and harder to understand. [M/JR/S86]

In some cases, students struggled throughout the semester to resolve their contradictory feelings about war. The one I remember best was Edward, a senior in the class I taught in spring 1986.

In a series of journal entries, Edward examined the origins and nature of what he called his "darker side," the part of him that found war fascinating, even attractive. He anticipated the focus for many of his journal entries in his first reflections on the course.

Expectations? Fears? What I expect to get out of the course is what I fear most. Of course, I hope to learn more than I already know about Vietnam. What I fear is learning more about myself. In this, I mean that I will see the darker side of my human nature. To understand the Vietnam experience, I must be able to mentally put myself in the boots of the grunts or whoever. This becomes scary if I start rationalizing the killings of others, and undoubtedly I will.

A few days later, Edward wrote that he had finished the first readings "just before the Superbowl." That conjunction of events led him to reflect on a disturbing connection between the war he had been reading about and the game he had just watched.

Football makes boys men. It's a macho sport. America loves it. The contact, the violence. . . . I know this doesn't have much to do with Vietnam, but after finishing a book where such destructive attitudes got totally out of hand, I found it scary to see similar mentalities applied to the game.

Many of Edward's reflections were evoked by everyday occurrences—TV shows, movies, incidents in his everyday life. In several of these journal entries, Edward tried to confront his contradictory feelings about violence and war. For example, in the following reflection on an occurrence in his fraternity house, Edward describes his reaction to watching a cat kill a mouse.

Something quite appropriate happened tonight. Our cat caught a mouse in our house. Like a bunch of goons, we stood around and watched him torment this poor, helpless animal for twenty minutes. He just plain taunted the thing. . . . While I felt sorry for the mouse, I loved it. It was exciting.

Another time, Edward reacted to the U.S. bombing of Khadafy's headquarters in Libya. Again, he analyzed his feelings—his "gut response" to the incident.

Boy, am I an idiot. I've just been wasting my time taking this class. Surprised? Well, it's true. Don't get me wrong. I've learned a great deal, it's fun, and I love it. But I realized today I'm wasting my time. I still haven't learned my lesson, the most important thing I should come away with. So what the heck am I talking about? Libya, of course. We bombed them yesterday. And you know my first reaction? My initial gut response? Yep, you guessed it. I was pleased. I thought, "Hot damn! Let's kick some ass. They're only a Third World country. They ain't got nothing on us. We're America." Then I stopped and thought about what I was just thinking. I thought about the same thing Caputo thought about Vietnam. It was then I realized that class really hasn't affected me the way I thought it had. I still had the same gut reaction.

Both kinds of reflections led him back to his ambivalent feelings about war. Immediately after his comments on the bombing of Libya, for example, Edward wrote:

I really wonder if I could kill somebody. On the one hand, I admit I have heroic fantasies about shooting hordes of the enemy (whoever they are). On the other, I see myself as a moralist, not wanting to kill or even get in a fight (I haven't been in a fight since second grade). I'm pulled in two different directions.

It wasn't clear whether Edward resolved his confusion, his feeling of being pulled in two directions, attracted to war and simultaneously repulsed by it. But he was able to examine his complex and contradictory responses with admirable honesty. At the end of the course, he wrote about the importance of this process of self-scrutiny.

For four years I've been taking courses here. Four years! And in that time, I've had one course that actually forced me to think about myself. . . . [In] the Vietnam course . . . you had to deal with yourself. You had to be honest, honest with you. One on one.

From the beginning of the semester, I tried to encourage students to be honest in expressing their reactions. Quite a few students claimed that the course helped them uncover their feelings and express their responses more candidly. As one freshman said: "Throughout this course I have found some feelings I did not know I had" [M/FR/F86]. A junior wrote that the course elicited "so many different emotions inside of me that I find it hard to explain them" [F/JR/S88]. By writing in their journals, students became more aware of how they felt, and in some cases, at least, the act of recording those responses seemed to elicit deeper feelings. When one of the freshmen looked back on the semester, she noted that at the beginning of the course she "was, in a way, out of touch with my emotions" [F/FR/F89]. Another student commented that her early entries lacked emotion, but that her writing changed as the course progressed:

In the first couple of journal entries, I seemed somewhat spiritless in my writing. Perhaps because I wasn't quite into the reading yet, but towards the end I was very into my entries. Often I would simply write down a quote and then go from there. Nevertheless, my writing seemed to mature during the semester. But actually, I think that it was myself that grew. . . . Reading over my journal was like looking in a mirror. [F/FR/F89]

Although the journal was the principal mechanism for exploring personal involvement, a few students found an outlet for their feelings through other media. Some were poets or musicians. And a couple of students were artists. One upperclassman took the course because he had been trying to paint about the war. And a student in my freshman course decided to work on an oil painting throughout the semester, using brush and canvas to express feelings that she "couldn't put into words."

I decided to paint a painting to reflect my feelings and emotions. . . . As the class grew in complexity so did my thoughts, which in turn were translated onto the canvas. Each stroke my brush made on the canvas was influenced directly or indirectly by the books we read. [F/FR/F89]

By encouraging involvement and expression, I hoped to deepen students' connections to the war, but I also wanted their responses to become better informed and increasingly reflective. One of the freshmen described quite clearly the process through which feelings developed into reflections: first she became more aware of her emotions and more willing to express them, then she found her emotional responses evolving into questions.

This type of entry helped me grow emotionally. The more I became receptive of my feelings, the more I could be receptive to the material we read, and vice versa. As I became more emotionally involved, my entries are taken over with questions. These questions enable me to develop my ideas. [F/FR/F86]

This dynamic interplay between emotional response and reflective questioning, between inquiries of the heart and mind, will continue to be a key topic in subsequent chapters.

At the end of a semester of reading, writing, and reflecting on the war, students often saw themselves as "veterans"—not only of a course about Vietnam, but veterans of an emotionally and intellectually intense experience.

Well, my tour of Vietnam has almost come to a close. I am what a Vietnam soldier would call a "short timer." I am soon to become a Vietnam veteran, and the experience of the war is a part of me now. [F/FR/F89]

Students had touched the war and it had touched them—imaginatively and vicariously, of course, but powerfully and significantly nonetheless.

I've felt what they were feeling, I've seen what they were seeing. . . . I've put myself in their shoes and realized how scared and lonely it must have been. In a fantastic way, I've been there. [F/FR/F89]

For students who had engaged in connected inquiry, the closing line of Michael Herr's *Dispatches* held special significance: "Vietnam Vietnam Vietnam, we've all been there" (278). "Yes," commented a freshman, "I believe we have" [F/FR/F86].

3 Literary Inquiry

Rather than looking at just the facts, the literature looks at the lives of the people involved in the facts. It is really the people involved who make up an event, and because of the approach literature takes, it is able to more truthfully get at what really happened at a particular event. This was a new and very exciting discovery for me. [F/JR/S88]

In his book *Dispatches*, Michael Herr, a correspondent for *Esquire* magazine, describes the intensity with which soldiers in the bush or on isolated fire bases would urge him to "tell it"—to tell readers what the soldiers were going through, to tell the truth about what it was like to fight in Vietnam. One time, during the bitter fighting in Hué, a Marine accosted Herr just as the writer was about to leave for the airstrip, issuing an impassioned charge:

Okay, man, you go on, you go on out of here you cocksucker, but I mean it, you tell it! You tell it, man. If you don't tell it. . . . (221)

My course was structured around a sequence of different types of writing about the Vietnam War: personal narratives, factual reports, novels, and sometimes poems. But whether "fact" or "fiction," traditional or unconventional, all of the books purported to "tell it," to represent what the war had been like and how it had affected the soldiers who were most deeply involved in it.

I decided to begin with accessible books and work toward more complex ones, bearing in mind that many of the students in my courses were drawn together by common requirements rather than by a common interest in the topic. Because they were more often draftees than volunteers, these students found the prospect of taking a literature course, especially one that involved a good deal of writing, about as appealing as basic training. And many of them viewed literature as a web of hidden meanings, abstract messages, and complex symbols, a puzzle that they had never been very good at solving. As one of the freshmen summarized her response to literary study: "Symbolism! Well, I have been bad at symbolism my entire literature career" [F/FR/F89].

Given these attitudes and orientations, I decided to start with students' experiences as readers—their felt responses to texts—rather than with principles and problems of literary interpretation. This approach to literature as experience owes a great deal to Louise Rosenblatt, who argued in her germinal book *Literature as Exploration* (first published in 1938) that literature is "something 'lived through,' something to which the student reacts on a variety of interrelated emotional and intellectual planes" (240). For Rosenblatt, the starting point for literary inquiry is an engaged response—a personally meaningful evocation of the work—although that response must eventually become the object of reflection and analysis.[1] As Rosenblatt says so cogently:

Though a free, uninhibited emotional reaction to a work of art or literature is an absolutely *necessary* condition of sound literary judgment, it is not . . . a *sufficient* condition. Without a real impact between the book and the mind of the reader, there can be no process of judgment at all, but honest recognition of one's own reaction is not in itself sufficient to insure sound critical opinion. . . . [A student] can begin to achieve a sound approach to literature only when he reflects upon his response to it, when

45

he attempts to understand what in the work and in himself produced that reaction, and when he thoughtfully goes on to modify, reject, or accept it. (75–76)

At the beginning of the course, I looked for sincerity and frankness in my students' reactions, agreeing with Rosenblatt that the basic measure of a student's response to a text should be "the genuineness of the ideas and reactions he expresses" (70). But I wanted to find ways to elicit more than emotional reactions, however sincere. One strategy was to deepen students' connections to the soldiers and their experiences, a process described in the previous chapter. The other strategy was to engage students in critical reflection, asking them to make comparative and evaluative judgments about a series of increasingly demanding texts. Thus I aimed for an approach that would not only support the "core of direct emotional experience at the heart of the critical process" (Rosenblatt 121), but would also challenge students to exercise reflective judgment.

Students' first opportunities for sustained literary inquiry came during the unit in which they read Philip Caputo's *Rumor of War* and Lynda Van Devanter's *Home Before Morning*. Although I designed the unit to facilitate comparative analysis (by having students read related parts of the memoirs together, such as home backgrounds, training, initiation to Vietnam, disillusionment with the war), I refrained from telling students exactly how to assess the two accounts. Instead, I strove to make the task of comparing these two memoirs an "open" problem: an assignment for which there was no simple algorithm and no single answer. I wanted students to voice their tacit principles of aesthetic judgment, to explore various evaluative strategies in group discussions and journal writing, and to work out their own criteria for assessing these two personal narratives.

From examining their journals and listening to their comments in class, I discovered that my students tended to focus on three criteria when they responded evaluatively to literature. The most frequently mentioned feature was the "intensity" of the writ-

46

ing—the extent to which it conveyed or elicited a strong emotional response. But that criterion was often intertwined with two others: the "authenticity" of the account (or the credibility of its author) and the "artistry" with which the story was told. Those three criteria remained central throughout the course, although their saliency changed: at the beginning of the semester, when students were reading personal narratives, claims about a book's intensity seemed to carry most weight, whereas issues of authenticity and especially artistry became increasingly significant later in the course.

Both memoirs elicited deep feelings, although students usually claimed that one was much more emotionally effective than the other. When they tried to explain why a particular memoir had elicited an intense emotional response, students tended to cite several features: the extent to which the account included dramatic and emotionally compelling episodes, the extent to which it revealed the writer's own deep feelings about those events, and the extent to which it represented the writer's attitudes toward other people or key personal relationships. Because Van Devanter's memoir had all of these features, most students agreed that she had written the account with the greatest emotional intensity.

Perhaps the most frequently cited feature of *Home Before Morning* was its dramatic and emotionally compelling scenes. In one of those episodes, Van Devanter finds a prom picture of "Gene and Katie" in the jacket of a dying soldier. A number of students commented on the extent to which they were moved by this incident.

Van Devanter . . . really rips your heart out and if she's trying to dig way down deep into the way you feel—she does a fantastic job. I cried. . . . the way Van Devanter talks about Gene, I mean here . . . she runs across this *person*, this person who has a family, a girlfriend—who maybe was a boy scout, went to church, school, got F's on his papers, loved his dog. A person who was just like her. . . . She picked up his leg and then she threw it away. Startling and how unbelievable to those who have never seen blood, flesh—pain. [F/FR/F86]

An intense memoir has compelling episodes, but it should also include the writer's own feelings about key events and relationships—or, in one student's words, writers of personal narratives should "get personal." Quite a few students preferred Van Devanter's account because she tended to reveal her deepest feelings, whereas, in the judgment of many students, Caputo did not.

Van Devanter was much more personal. She let us know the people she knew. Caputo, on the other hand, does not let us get to know his characters on a personal basis. . . . That seems to be a major difference between the two books. To me, *Home Before Morning* is more interesting because it is so personal. [F/FR/F86]

Van Devanter . . . tells more, makes you feel like her confidant. A book should do that and let you see what makes this person tick. . . . [In Caputo] the story and writing are good, but the sight of the inner person is cloudy or somewhat disguised. [M/FR/F86]

Moreover, Van Devanter focused more attention on human relationships, in the students' view. As one freshman put it:

I think we, as readers, get to know Lynda better than we get to know Mr. Caputo. We know Lynda through her relationships with others. In *A Rumor of War* we don't get to know Caputo's friends. He keeps us at a distance. [F/FR/F86]

Even the difference in reference—to "Lynda" but to "Mr. Caputo"—reveals how close this student feels to Van Devanter, how distant from Caputo.

Most students agreed that Caputo had adopted a more "distanced" approach to his book, using techniques that gave his narrative the feel of an "objective" account of his experiences, whereas Van Devanter had taken a more "personal" approach, writing in a more "subjective" way about her feelings and relationships. While students sometimes argued about which approach was more appropriate and effective, the majority seemed to feel that Caputo's restrained account was less successful than Van Devanter's straightforwardly emotional approach.

Although students often focused on the criterion of intensity when comparing the two books, they also considered the *authenticity* of the authors' accounts. One reason that so many of them focused on the matter of authenticity was, I suspect, because I had encouraged them to respond critically to the oral histories with which we began the course. In that first unit, I urged students to ask some hard questions about the validity of soldiers' stories, considering their limitations and sources of bias (a topic I will consider more fully in the next chapter). Some of that skepticism carried over to the students' reading of the memoirs, as I hoped it would. But what interested me most was the fact that Caputo's memoir tended to receive more critical scrutiny than Van Devanter's book. In general, students expressed two kinds of doubts about the credibility of *A Rumor of War*. Some students were suspicious about the many specific details: they worried that Caputo had reconstructed a good many "facts," or perhaps even fabricated them.

Another criticism . . . is that, in my opinion, Caputo remembers *too much*. I cannot see how anyone could remember as many details as Caputo did. I'm sure he filled in some blanks of his memory with someone else's story or what *could have* happened. [F/FR/F86]

Other students were more concerned about Caputo's motives for writing his memoir: it was clear to quite a few of them that he did not write the book merely to tell readers what the war was like for a young Marine officer in 1965. Rather, Caputo appears to have told his story to figure out how he had become the kind of person who could participate—even if indirectly—in the killing of an innocent South Vietnamese boy. Or perhaps he was writing to explain his actions, or even to justify them. In the following journal entry, we see a freshman's emerging sense that Caputo is controlling his narrative, manipulating the reader.

Caputo is trying to set something up, prepare the reader for something that will not be made clear until the very end. . . . Something seems strange about the course of Caputo's writing, though I can't quite put my finger on it. . . . It's as if the events and how they are told are too structured and preplanned— shaped and conformed for a special reason. Everything is building up for an insightful or "surprising" ending. [M/FR/F86]

On the other hand, Van Devanter's book elicited surprisingly little reflection concerning its authenticity. Many students appeared to believe that the intensity of Van Devanter's memoir was a reliable index of its sincerity, and hence its truthfulness and trustworthiness.

I enjoyed Lynda Van Devanter's account of Vietnam perhaps more than anything else we've read. She seems to be very truthful, mostly because of the emotion she uses in writing. [F/FR/F86]

A few students even went so far as to claim that intensity of feeling precluded or prevented critical reflection. As one student said, "I hardly want to think about the book—it just makes me sad" [F/FR/F86]. Another wrote that she found it "very hard to criticize . . . because I was too wrapped up in the story" [F/FR/F86]. The potency of Van Devanter's story rendered at least some students powerless to analyze or evaluate her account. And some of them seemed to equate critical assessment with *criticism* of the author. In the case of *Home Before Morning*, students were reluctant to make any statements that could be construed as criticisms of a woman with whom they so deeply empathized.[2]

I think it's OK to question the stories a little but not put them down. Van Devanter went through hell and for us to constantly cut her down because of the way she writes is wrong. [F/FR/F89]

Conversely, students tended to view Caputo's memoir with suspicion, in part because he was more restained in expressing his emotions. As one freshman put it: "Sometimes I felt the book was a fake because there was no emotion" [F/FR/F86]. A number of students focused on the section in *A Rumor of War* in which Caputo learns about the death of his friend, Walter Levy. These students not only criticize Caputo for what they see as an unfeeling response to his friend's death, but they also take Caputo's lack of emotional intensity as grounds for distrusting his narrative, grounds for doubting its authenticity.

When Levy dies, Caputo states that he is upset but he doesn't show or tell his emotions. He tries to explain what a great guy Levy was but it lacks emotions. Either Caputo is hiding something or not willing to show his real feelings. It makes me question his credibility. . . . A reader has to believe the author and understand his feelings before they trust his credibility. To really understand a book you have to get into it and feel something for the characters. With Caputo's lack of emotion I couldn't get interested in his book or his characters. This left me with a lack of trust in his stories. [F/FR/F86]

Thus students' assessments of the emotional intensity of a memoir were frequently bound up with their judgments about the authenticity of the account or the credibility of the author's claims. For most students, Van Devanter's involved, confessional approach was evidence that she was being honest and telling the truth, whereas Caputo's more detached and analytical approach suggested dishonesty and deception.

At first glance, this interwoven quality of students' judgments might appear to be exactly what I have said I was after in the course: I wanted to promote heartfelt reflection, an integration of thought and feeling. But what I hoped to foster was a more complex matrix for literary evaluation, one in which the voices of both response and reflection, both heart and mind, would be heard. What some of my students (especially some of the freshmen) seemed to lack was an ability to listen to both voices at the same time. When they could still their hearts—as many of them did with *A Rumor of War*—they could become more critical, considering the authenticity of an account. But when they felt intense empathy for the author and deep engagement in her story—as most did with *Home Before Morning*—they seemed to listen only to their hearts, forcing their judgments to conform with their responses. A freshman put it succinctly: "the memoirs . . . opened my heart and closed my mind" [F/FR/F86].

When they were asked to assess the memoirs, students most often focused on intensity and authenticity. But a third criterion was sometimes involved in students' literary judgments: the author's *artistry*. Most students agreed that a "good" book should include techniques that engage a reader's interest and attention. But on the question of which features or whose techniques best promoted engagement, there were disagreements. Quite a few students found Caputo to be verbose, excessively "literary," and "boring" because of long passages of description and detail.

Caputo used a lot of fancy words and terms, making it very literary but not too believable. [F/FR/F86]

How do you convey a largely boring segment of time without being boring? I think Caputo tries to overcome this by using more descriptive language. Sometimes I just don't think this works. [M/SR/S86]

Or as one student pointedly expressed her reaction:

I am *so* bored! Caputo is driving me crazy! He goes on and on about details so much that I completely drift off while I'm read-ing. There isn't anything to keep me interested! Hardly ever does he talk about his feelings or the others' feelings. It is so hard to keep my attention on this book! . . . Why doesn't this guy put some feeling into it? He frustrates me so much! . . . I can't under-stand why this book is *so* raved over. [F/FR/F86]

But there were also dissenting voices. Some students were attracted to the very features that repelled many of their peers— Caputo's use of detailed description and metaphor.

This account by Caputo is so well written I could actually feel the anticipation, the heat, smell the stench of Vietnam. Caputo truly is a master of simile and metaphor. His description of the night—the blinding, fearful night—the night that put Americans in a defensive position. A territory unknown became a monster at nightfall—sniper fire, phantom fire, interrupted. I just wanted to take this time to comment on how well written I think this book is. Caputo actually lets me see into his mind. [F/JR/S86]

Another dissenting view was that Van Devanter's writing was "almost like one of those Harlequin romance books" [F/SO/S88]. And for those students, there were questions about how far Van Devanter's account could be trusted. As the student who compared *Home Before Morning* to a Harlequin romance said: "I can't help but doubt the truth in it."

I tried to encourage those minority views and draw out dissenting judgments during class discussions. Nevertheless, most of my students preferred Van Devanter's style of writing, with its emotional episodes, its focus on people and relationships, and its unadorned style, to Caputo's artful ruminations on killing and dying. The consensus in every class I taught was that Caputo's book was difficult and pretentious, and that those qualities somehow confirmed suspicions about Caputo's lack of sincerity and authenticity. Conversely, most students viewed Van Devanter's memoir as a personal, accessible, and therefore trustworthy account of a young woman's difficult year in Vietnam.[3]

The memoirs provided an engaging project with which to begin literary inquiry, but in fact neither of the personal narratives afforded much of a challenge to students' interpretive strategies or ways of reading. In subsequent units, therefore, I sought to confront students with more complex texts, books that violated their assumptions about "good writing" and challenged their strategies of literary inquiry. My aim, as Rosenblatt says so well, was to foster students' "capacity to undertake rewarding relationships with increasingly demanding texts" (*The Reader* 140). And the first of those demanding texts was Michael Herr's *Dispatches*.

When students began reading *Dispatches* many of them were
perplexed and bewildered.

It was just like we were thrown right into the middle of everything without any warning. . . . I'm having a hard time writing
this entry because the opening section left me with no lasting
impression. I felt confused and lost. [F/SR/S88]

Rather than telling a straightforward story or providing a chronological report, Herr presents a collage of musings and memories,
a collection of apparently unrelated stories and reflections that
seemed to make the Vietnam experience less comprehensible
and left many students confused.

I've begun reading Herr's *Dispatches* and my first reaction is that
it caught me off guard. I was expecting more traditional writing,
maybe a story. [M/SR/S86]

Quite a few students focused on the fact that the opening section
of *Dispatches* (titled "Breathing In") is not organized chronologically, and they realized that Herr's nonlinear presentation, or
what some referred to as a "lack of organization," was causing
them problems.

"Breathing In," I think, is a lot different from what we have been
reading. It isn't arranged chronologically at all. It seems like Herr
is just writing things down as he remembers them. To me it
doesn't seem like there is any order to it. . . . It's pretty difficult
to read because I really can't read it swiftly and pick up on what
it's saying. [F/FR/F86]

For a few students, the demands of the book were so great
that they could not keep reading. One junior was particularly
forthright about her frustration.

I tried to finish *Dispatches*. But I couldn't. . . . I think I got tired
of having to read so much and so carefully. It was not an easy
book to read and took a lot of concentration and dedication to
read it. I got behind and never really caught up. . . . That's too

bad, I realize, but that's the way I felt and that's probably why I couldn't finish. [F/JR/S88]

But most students persevered. I tried to encourage students to stick with the book by exhibiting my own enthusiastic response to it. As one of the upperclassmen wrote at midterm:

Most striking is your obvious enthusiasm for the material. Believe it or not, when I started reading *Dispatches*, I was rather bored. After a class of watching you rant and rave about it (plus giving us a context to read it in—i.e., new journalism), I went back and began to get a lot more out of it. [M/JR/S86]

Although my "ranting and raving" was important for some students, many more of them found that the journal writing helped them make sense of their responses to *Dispatches*. In fact, the journals became increasingly valuable when students had to reckon with a difficult text. One of the freshmen put it well:

At the beginning of the semester, I did not like the idea of having to write down how I was reacting to the works that I was reading. I really felt it was going to be a waste of time. I really started to change how I felt about the journals while I was reading Michael Herr's book, *Dispatches*. Because *Dispatches* is rather disjointed, it takes a while to understand why some of the sections are put where they are and in that order. The journal really helped me because I was able to write what I thought each section was trying to convey to the reader. [F/FR/F86]

With encouragement, most students began to understand not only why they found this book so confusing but also why Herr might have employed an unconventional method of writing.

What the hell is Herr's point? When I look back on what I read, I can't seem to recall much. Little bits and pieces thrown at the reader. I'm lost—yet I feel as though in being lost, I found what Herr wanted me to. He wanted me to say "What the hell's going on?" He wants the reader to be confused. Because by creating that state of mind—confusion, uncertainty, lost—he is doing what I as a reader want him to do, which is let me know what it was like in Vietnam. [M/FR/F89]

The crisis passed for some students when they realized that they could approach *Dispatches*, despite its unconventional features, with familiar criteria of judgment: intensity, authenticity, and artistry. In fact, what rescued many students from their initial despair was the intensity of their experience with the text. The students' journals are full of comments about the book's capacity to engage them in the Vietnam experience—or, in a student's words, "*Dispatches* . . . kind of sucks you into the war" [F/JR/S86]. For many students, the book soon became a powerful experience. A junior claimed he had "never experienced such an emotional outpouring from reading a book" [M/JR/S88]. A senior reported having had a series of dreams about the book: "I know it sounds weird, but I'd wake fatigued. . . . I felt that I not only read the book, but experienced it as well" [M/SR/S86]. And in the following journal entry, a freshman offers a vivid account of why she found the book so compelling.

This book is intense. It just seems like a series of words and emotions, one shotgunning out after another. The stories are amazing and so brutal. Herr holds nothing back. The story about the Marine pissing in the open mouth of a dead NVA—is shocking. His writing is intense, one pulse after another—a solid stream of fact/emotions—it's as if he leads the reader over and lifts a dark blanket and *forces* the reader to look at something horrible and disgusting, something shunned and denied, and every time you want to turn away or twist away in horror—Herr grabs you by the back of the head and forces you to look. [F/FR/F86]

Many students commented on the intensity and emotional power of Herr's stories and short anecdotes—stories which, in one student's words, "made my eyes pop out of my skull when I read them" [M/FR/F86]. The journals were full of notes about those memorable anecdotes.

The guy who couldn't leave Khe Sanh—sitting on his duffle bag forever, like in Herr's mind he's still there twiddling his thumbs. . . . The guy with the months of his tour on his flack jacket— dead the month before he was to leave. The way Herr has us read each month, the feeling really sticks. . . . The part with Mayhew extending his tour—crazy, yeah, but there is this attitude of "who really wants to go back to the States 'cause the system's fucked." . . . Mayhew watching Vietnam like a kid at a scary movie—very good allegory, scared yet deeply involved and fascinated—Herr has a way of writing [so] that I can see the look on the faces of his characters. [M/JR/S86]

While many students commented on the power of Herr's stories, others asserted that the intensity of *Dispatches* came from the metaphoric language, colorful images, unusual turns of phrase, and fresh descriptions—Herr's *artistry*, in short.

One of Herr's great achievements is his ability to capture the language of the men who fought in Vietnam, using the words of common soldiers, whom one student described as the "sick, tired, superstitious, bad-mouthed grunts" [F/JR/S86]. It was a raw, vulgar language that seems to capture the essence of the Vietnam experience.

The language . . . *drives* at you and expresses points that can't be made by using ordinary words. [Example passage.] It's not the fact that all the cuss words attracted me to this. It's how they are used. The "f" word has such a *strong* feeling behind it. It just lets you know how scary it really was. I could feel the words being yelled at me. [F/FR/F89]

Many students copied out passages that they found particularly striking although, as one student said, "When I read a really good description, I feel like writing it down, but it would take forever to do that in this book!!" [F/SO/S88]. Students' journals were full of commentary on passages that impressed them:

His writing style is a little off the wall too. Especially when he describes things. I mean, how can you have "an old story with hair still growing on it"? Yet, I know what he means and his

technique is very effective. Herr can also create images with quite
an impact in just one sentence. "The eyes going wider than the
eyes of horses caught in a fire." That's pretty wide! [F/FR/F86]

I had to put *Dispatches* down when he talked about combat being
like making love to a girl for the first time. . . . It just stopped
me, sent my mind flying. That was all I could read that day. [M/
FR/F86]

I marked some passages that really stood out for me. . . . "their
secret brutalized them and darkened them and very often it made
them beautiful. It took no age, seasoning or education to make
them know exactly where true violence resided." This could be
a poem. [M/SR/S86]

The sound of "closet throat stickers"—just saying it makes my
throat [feel] clammy and unprotected. [M/JR/S86]

The detail Herr uses just grabs you and pulls you into it. "I felt
a cold fat drop of sweat start down the middle of my back like a
spider. . . ." I really did feel it. I even tried to wipe it away. [F/
FR/F89]

Despite their initial reservations, most of the students I taught
came to judge *Dispatches* as one of the best books they had read
in the course.

When I first started reading *Dispatches* I really didn't like it,
basically because I didn't understand it. . . . But as I finish up
the last two parts of *Dispatches* I realize it has turned into my
favorite book so far. It's so original and it makes you answer
your own questions and makes you think. [F/FR/F86]

And the major reason that students found the book so compelling
was that Herr was an artist who could tell stories in a fresh and
provocative way.

How does he do it? His intensity and depth of understanding
permeate this book. This book seeps with meaning. . . . His
feelings are so tangible. . . . He expressed himself so well that
he makes me feel like I experienced what he did. . . . He is an

artist. His words are like vivid pictures. . . . All I know is that this is one great work of art. [M/FR/F89]

In terms of intensity and artistry, *Dispatches* got high marks. But what about authenticity? Was Herr a credible author? Was his account believable? Did he find a way to "tell it?" Such questions go to the heart of the book, because Herr claims that traditional journalistic methods were simply inadequate for the war in Vietnam, so that he had to develop an alternative kind of writing and reporting. Herr is quite critical of many of his fellow correspondents, too many of whom were content to rely on secondhand accounts of the war—worst of all, on briefings by military officials, briefings which focused on the "facts" of operations and produced a wealth of statistics, but which obscured the reality of the war as it was actually being fought. To such "objective" methods of fact-gathering, Herr contraposed methods of participant observation: living with combat soldiers—the "grunts"—and seeing the war through their eyes.[4]

With few exceptions, students accepted Herr's critique of conventional journalism as well as his claims for an alternative mode of investigative reporting. Karen is a good example: like many of her peers, she trusted Herr because he was so deeply committed to getting his story, even to the point of exposing himself to combat. As Karen put it: "I also tend to trust Herr and what he tells us simply because he is there with these grunts in Vietnam— willingly and devotedly." Because of Herr's deep involvement, most students believed that his account of the war was trustworthy and authentic—the real story.

Out of all the books we've read so far, I felt that *Dispatches* was the truest one. [F/JR/S88]

Giving 110 percent to his stories, Michael Herr accomplished his task of relating to us the real story of Vietnam. [F/FR/F86]

This book, more than any other we've read, rings true. It seems to tell how it really was for the men fighting the war. [F/JR/S88]

Herr's authenticity rests in part on his participatory style of reporting. But students gave additional reasons to consider Herr a trustworthy author. For example, Karen pointed out that Herr is honest about his limitations and forthright about his fallibility: she can "admire Herr's honesty" because he confesses that "sometimes he didn't know if something took place in a second or in an hour or if he simply dreamed it." This admission sets Herr apart from the other authors she has read:

In previous accounts that we have read, I do not remember the authors admitting they could be mistaken. What they say happened could have been a mere construction in their own minds. . . . Because Herr recognizes this, [it] gives him more credit—the Vietnam he portrays seems more accurate, more believable because I know he has wrestled with himself to determine what really happened, not just what he thought or possibly dreamt happened.

In addition, Karen noted that Herr is troubled about his role and reflective about the status of his account.

The fact that one can tell through his words that Herr is going through a personal conflict about his experiences in Vietnam not only makes me admire him but it makes me truly believe and trust him. He doesn't simply accept what happened and what he witnessed at face value—he examines his thoughts, his feelings, his memories.

Other students also pointed out ways in which Herr is reflective about his role and his responsibilities. For example, he is aware that because the line between participant and observer is very fine, he is implicated in the war and responsible for the events he watches. Many students were struck by the idea that a reporter could consider himself accountable for what he observes.

I looked over the book again and found the line, "You were as responsible for everything you saw as you were for everything you did." I think this is the most disturbing thing for Herr. He feels as responsible for the war as those fighting it. [F/FR/F86]

Students accepted Herr's self-critical attitude and awareness of moral responsibility as a sign of his authenticity and trustworthiness. As Karen said, "When you know that someone is struggling to discover the 'truth,' you develop a respect for that person." And most students agreed with the freshman who claimed that "Herr's book is as close to Vietnam as our generation will ever get" [F/FR/F86].

The experience of reading *Dispatches* was important for my students because it asked them to work with a demanding literary text. Although the book caused a brief period of disorientation, students soon found that they could assess Herr's achievement by using the same criteria they had applied to the memoirs. And yet, in applying those familiar criteria—intensity, authenticity, artistry—to this text, the relationships among the three criteria of judgment began to shift. Intensity and emotional involvement were still basic, but intensity had less influence on judgments of Herr's authenticity than it had when students worked on the memoirs, where emotionality was often synonymous with sincerity. With *Dispatches*, judgments of authenticity depended on other signs of the author's credibility, especially the writer's reflectiveness: students tended to trust Herr because he confessed that "telling it" was inherently difficult and problematic.

Also, questions of artistry assumed greater importance with *Dispatches*, and many more students cited specific language, images, or metaphors as the basis for their engagement with the text. In short, this unconventional and challenging text gave students an opportunity to extend literary inquiry and to focus on aesthetic concerns.

I always followed *Dispatches* with a unit that encouraged students to pursue reflection on issues of artistry and aesthetic judgment. In most cases I moved directly to war fiction, but in one of the freshman courses I paused for a one-week unit on poetry, asking students to read Yusef Komunyakaa's collection *Dien Cai Dau* (which means "crazy" in Vietnamese). A number of students immediately saw the connection between Herr and Komunyakaa: both writers create intensity through their art- istry—by manipulating language, image, and detail.

[Komunyakaa] does the same thing that Michael Herr does with imagery. He connects one thought to another and flows by a series of associations. [M/FR/F89]

I expected that because students had enjoyed the language and imagery in *Dispatches*, they would be prepared to appreciate the poems in *Dien Cai Dau*. What I did not anticipate, however, was their thoroughly negative attitude toward poetry: for many of these freshmen, the idea of reading poetry was a distasteful and distressing prospect.

The reason it was difficult for me to read *Dien Cai Dau* . . . was the haunting truth that it was poetry—the most intimidating six- letter word ever. Poetry is hard for me to read. [F/FR/F89]

I have always, *always* hated, just hated, to read poetry. I can't understand what the author is trying to say. I always need a teacher to tell me what he means and what the theme is. [M/FR/ F89]

Another common complaint was that poetry was "deep," full of symbols and hidden meanings, a complex puzzle to which students lacked the key.

Poetry to me has always been foreign. I could read a poem and try to figure out what it meant, but I never could get the deep meaning. [F/FR/F89]

Poetry, to me, is a mystery. No one can say what is right or wrong. It is impossible to tell what exactly a poet is trying to say. [M/FR/F89]

Even Karen, who claimed to like poetry and to be good at deci- phering its meanings and messages, confessed that "even after thinking, I cannot always see the underlying messages of a poem."

Given these negative sentiments and downright hostile attitudes, *Dien Cai Dau* faced an unreceptive audience. Because he is a colleague who teaches in my department, I invited Komunyakaa to read some poems and answer students' questions during one of the classes, hoping that his presence would change students' attitudes.

Today in lecture Yusef Komunyakaa came and read his poetry. . . . It was really cool because when he read them it was like they came alive. The room was just totally silent and when he read the words, it was like his expressions and his voice told a whole other story. It was just like the poems came alive. I just can't explain how it felt. [F/FR/F89]

If anyone hates poetry more than me, step forward. I despised it in high school and dreaded it this week, but Komunyakaa really changed my mind about it. I could honestly follow a lot of the themes. The words were great! [M/FR/F89]

For many students, the most important discovery was simply that good poetry is not necessarily "deep" and complex. Komunyakaa's verse is compact and imagistic, but also lucid and accessible. And those qualities impressed students who equated poetry with obscurity.

The thing that I learned was that the emotion and feeling put into poetry by the writer does not have to be extremely complicated. . . . I've realized that poetry isn't some incredible complicated thing I will never grasp. [Komunyakaa] made me realize I can grasp his poetry and emotion. . . . I now have confidence in my ability to read poetry in general. [M/FR/F89]

Although we spent only a week on *Dien Cai Dau*, the unit gave students an important opportunity to discover that a poet could "tell it," too: telling it in a way that created intensity and evoked deep feelings, not by relating grisly tales but by verbal artistry, by manipulating symbols and images.

Therefore, by the time they finished the poetry unit, students were ready to rephrase the questions that had guided their literary inquiry, asking not just who had managed to "tell it" truly and powerfully, but who had found a way to "tell it" freshly and artfully, without cliché. Good writing had to be authentic, and it had to convey something of the intensity of the Vietnam experience. But war stories—even true ones—get old fast, dulling the senses and blunting their impact. Some students realized that the kinds of stories that shocked them early in the course no longer moved them to tears of anger or sorrow.

The stories were no longer different. They began looking like a form letter with only a few of the characteristics changed. . . . You can only read such powerful material for so long before it has a negative effect. [M/FR/F89]

Boredom. As I continued to study the different books, I saw that I was reading the same story over and over. The authors were different . . . yet each story expressed the same emotions, the same gripping details of war, the same horror that the Vietnam War brought. [F/FR/F89]

The poetry had surprised students, dispelling some of their boredom with war stories. Could the fictional narratives be as compelling?

In the two classes I taught for upperclassmen, I asked students to read a pair of novels: James Webb's *Fields of Fire* and Tim O'Brien's *Going After Cacciato*. I hoped that these very different books would give students a fresh context for inquiring into issues of style and narrative approach. But in the freshman courses, where I was always pressed for time, I asked students to read only one novel—O'Brien's. Both approaches worked well, although I found that students who had read Webb's book first were better prepared to see O'Brien's complex tale as a particularly sophisticated achievement.

Most of my students understood Webb's novel as an effort to portray, as realistically as possible, the kind of men who fought the war and the kind of conflict they faced in Vietnam. Students recognized that Webb, a highly decorated Vietnam veteran, was trying to "tell it" the way it was. But for the most part, students felt that Webb lacked skill as a novelist, and that *Fields* was like a "soap opera" or a "made-for-TV movie" with flat characters and a corny plot.[5]

Fields of Fire is very predictable. I find myself looking at the next page for "BOOM" or "CRACK" when there is a scene where a patrol is in the woods. Nine times out of ten there it is on the next page. Webb lets the reader know what's coming up a mile away. [M/SR/S86]

Characters, too, impressed them as shallow and stereotypic.

The characters are so stereotyped that it's laughable. It's not that the situations are unreal, I guess it's just that the dialogue seems forced. [M/SR/S86]

Students felt that Webb had sacrificed a good story in his effort to portray a full cross-section of characters, acting in a complete range of situations.

It's an average novel, very predictable and certainly full of clichés. It does give a fairly good overview as to the many situations and characters that were involved in the Vietnam War, but it does all this at the expense of the plot. [M/SR/S86]

In addition, a number of students were critical of certain attitudes and values that they thought were expressed in the book. Some students felt that Webb was conveying a macho-militaristic message. Others noticed that few of the characters in the book are at all reflective about the war or their participation in it, the sole exception being the Harvard-educated misfit, Will Goodrich, who is the stereotype of a man for whom reflection precludes action. And quite a few students—especially, although not exclusively, women—noticed that all of the female characters in the

book are portrayed unsympathetically, as weak-willed objects of
men's pleasure. Their comments are worth quoting at length.

I did not especially appreciate the reputation several of the
women in this book had. For starters, Snake's mother was an
old, desperate whore who could barely move around the apart-
ment—worthless. Hodges' mother was a wimpering shadow of
a woman, cowering behind Hodges' stepfather while hiding her
true love in a green trunk. Then Mitsuko, the girl Hodges falls
in love with—what a wimp—she has no backbone, "Oh, I don't
know"—she would say "no" to Hodges and then go and do it!
. . . And then the description of Bagger's cheerleader wife as
an animal—a seductress. . . . And then the young Vietnamese
whore and the animalistic description of her as she brings Bagger
to feel guilty and dirty in his indulgence. . . . All the women are
feeble and animal-like. All are negative influences on the male
world. Webb obviously feels war is a male bonding that must be
tightened against any female influence; therefore, he does not
allow the females to be strong characters. [F/JR/S86]

There's something that bothers me about the women in *Fields of
Fire*. Webb makes it sound like they're all animals underneath.
Horny and easy. Mitsuko surrendered her virginity very easily
to Hodges (she must've had hundreds of propositions from Marines; why did she choose him?). The Vietnamese woman was
supposedly overcome with her animalistic urges when she had
sex with Dan. A cheerleader, with the "animal in her" (244),
seduces Bagger ("left tackle marries pregnant cheerleader." In
Georgia. It's *too* clichéd). And a horny fifteen-year-old girl seduces Cat Man (Cat Boy?) when he's only thirteen. Come on!
Webb's image of women in general is so unreal. He makes it
sound like they're all whores. Even Snake's mother is a nympho,
as well as a girl passenger in a car that picks up Sgt. Gilliland in
California. Only in the movies (especially of the James Bond
genre) are women so easily seduced because underneath they're
animals. The true beauty of woman is discarded by Webb. To
him they're only animals in heat, at any age. The erotic passages
in this book are almost boring, they're so similar. [M/SR/S86]

Although many of the students responded negatively to *Fields
of Fire*—and some even recommended that in "the next Vietnam

class you instruct do not include *Fields*" [F/JR/S86]—by the end
of the unit I was convinced that the novel had provided students
with an important opportunity to exercise literary judgment, and
that it had been useful for them to examine a flawed book after
reading *Dispatches*, a brilliant one. Moreover, *Fields of Fire* set the
stage for *Going After Cacciato*: having seen some limitations of a
traditional novel, students would be more receptive, I hoped, to
the possibilities of an alternative way of writing fiction.

I'm about a quarter of the way through *Cacciato* tonight, and I
must say that out of all the works we've read so far, I find this
one the most enjoyable. I feel that Tim O'Brien is the most
talented of the authors. Especially after reading *Fields of Fire*.
James Webb really annoyed me. His style, themes, and plot
were very forced and unnatural. Nothing really seemed to flow.
Reading Webb was more like watching a B movie. He was so
predictable and overt it's sickening. On the other hand, O'Brien
is an artist. [M/SR/S86]

As one student concluded: "Unconventional wars required unconventional novels (or reports) I guess" [M/SR/S86]. Nevertheless, *Going After Cacciato* would tax even the best students' toler-
ance for the unconventional.

The main plot of *Going After Cacciato*—desertion and pursuit—
seems straightforward enough. But O'Brien tells this story by
interweaving three narrative strands: Berlin's ruminations, especially on the role of imagination, as he stands guard in a watch-
tower from midnight until dawn (the "Observation Post" chapters); stories from Berlin's memory, especially his memory of
events that led to the deaths of his comrades (the "Memory"
chapters); and a bizarre and magical tale in which Berlin and his
unit chase Cacciato from the jungles of Vietnam to the streets of
Paris (the "Journey" chapters). Students found it challenging
just to unravel the three strands. The freshmen were especially
perplexed.

This has got to be the hardest . . . assignment yet. . . . The
reading is easy but the way it is organized is confusing. . . . As

I read I get confused on which lieutenant was alive and which lieutenant was dead. The book is organized strangely. People die in one chapter and are alive in another one. [F/FR/F86]

Because the going was rough, I produced reading guides and provided discussion questions, devices I rarely used during other units. I also devoted some lectures to exploring ways of reading and interpreting *Cacciato*. And I tried to find some tricks to keep students interested in this difficult book. For example, when we were reading about the fragging of Lt. Sidney Martin, I passed around a grenade (a dummy), asking students to "touch it," just as the squad members had done to secure everyone's assent. One student said that she was "kinda nervous" when I brought out the grenade:

I knew that it could no longer explode, but yet I still had a weird feeling. I also could see Paul Berlin and the others touching the grenade that would soon kill the lieutenant. This may sound weird, but I was kinda wondering that if I touched the grenade being passed around, then I was saying it was all right to kill the lieutenant. I didn't like that feeling at all. [F/FR/F86]

And when we read about how Cacciato's habit of chewing Black Jack gum resulted in licorice-scented conversations on a night patrol, I passed out sticks of chewing gum.

Today in class was really interesting. First of all, we talked about Cacciato and Paul Berlin and the incident when Cacciato was chewing Black Jack gum. When I read this part in the book I tried to imagine the scene and smell of the gum. . . . When Prof. Kroll passed out Black Jack gum to all of us, it gave me an image of what was going on at the time. I smelled the smell of licorice, just as Paul Berlin did. It's amazing how one thing (like gum) can just set you right in the scene. [F/FR/F86]

Once students persevered long enough to get caught up in the story, most of them were hooked. In the following journal entry, for example, a senior traces his evolving response.

Literary Inquiry

The more I read *Going After Cacciato* the stranger I feel. In the beginning of the book I thought this imaginary journey was a bit ridiculous, and I kept thinking, well how could they get up and leave, how could they pay for it all, how could they go through all these countries? Why didn't they just take a plane and hit Paris? It just seemed ridiculous. The more I read the more I'm getting engulfed by the whole journey. It is like turning to the next chapter and hoping it's one on the journey. Then all of a sudden you read some of the memory part and you get all caught up in that. . . . Then we hit a part on the Observation Post and you enjoy that. So all of a sudden two hundred and some odd pages into the book you are really enjoying it and in a weird sort of way it makes sense. . . . It's frustrating and mind boggling, but then it's also great. It's a piece of art. [M/SR/S86]

While many of the episodes on the journey to Paris are bizarre and surreal, students were particularly intrigued by the first of the strange occurrences, an incident in which the squad and their Vietnamese companion, Sarkin Aung Wan, suddenly fall through a "hole in the road," descending magically into a VC tunnel complex, occupied by a lone North Vietnamese major, Li Van Hgoc. Some students had difficulty accepting this episode or understanding what it could possibly signify.

I mean—honestly! I'm sure that an earthquake would all of the sudden just pop up and they would "accidentally" fall into the tunnel. None of them were even hurt in the fall through the cracks in the earth. Also, it took them forever to get out. How did they get there in the first place? Couldn't they crawl out the same hole that they fell in? Or did the earth suddenly close back up again? How real is that anyway? That's bizarre! [F/FR/F86]

Like so many of the incidents in the book, this scene is both real and unreal, and it calls for multiple levels of analysis and interpretation. On one level, the scene portrays well the frustrations of fighting an enemy who can live underground, melting into the earth. Moreover, the tunnel scene connects this event in the imaginary journey with Berlin's recollection of important events from his tour—in particular, a period during which the squad is forced to search tunnels, resulting in the death of two of their comrades and leading them to rebel against their platoon leader, whom they eventually kill, presumably by dropping a grenade into a tunnel he is searching. This connection is quite explicit: when Berlin looks through a periscope in Li Van Hgoc's tunnel, he apparently sees his squad getting ready to search a tunnel complex.

When they are down in the tunnel with the NVA deserter and Paul Berlin is looking into the periscope, he sees figures and somebody looking into a hole but he cannot make it out. Li Van Hgoc says, "Look closer. Concentrate." Is he seeing the scene that takes place in the next chapter? [M/SR/S86]

They looked through the periscope and saw the "reality" part of the story. . . . Wow. [M/FR/F86]

Trapped in the tunnel complex, the squad tries to find a way out. The key lies in a riddle that Sarkin Aung Wan recites: "The way in is the way out. We have fallen into a hole, now we must fall out." The squad follows Sarkin, and when they emerge from the tunnels they come out of a manhole in the streets of Mandalay. The episode baffled some students.

The chapter where the platoon falls in a hole and meets the VC in the tunnels really blew me away. I had a hard time following what was going on, especially when the Vietnamese girl was trying to explain how to exit the tunnels. She says, "the way in is the way out." . . . I don't understand what she's getting at. Maybe it isn't supposed to make sense. [F/SR/S88]

But others tried to find significance in the tunnel scene.

The squad's falling in the hole is one of the strangest events in the book. In a similar way, the United States fell into the Vietnam War. Just like Berlin's squad, the U.S. got into something that was absurd and confusing. The tunnel that both the squad and the U.S. fell into was a system of mazes and confusion. It seemed like there was no way to get out. . . . Unfortunately, the U.S.

didn't have an adviser with the insight of Sarkin Aung Wan. As she said, "the way in is the way out. We have fallen into a hole, now we must fall out." [M/FR/F86]

Because *Cacciato* is replete with these kinds of provocative and multilayered episodes, it seemed to elicit a special kind of reflection, a more exploratory, speculative, and interpretive response than I saw in other units of the course. A number of students used their journals to explore the book's central meanings.

I want to explore the possibility that Paul Berlin actually wanted to desert and was using his imagination to figure out how. Pretty farfetched, huh? . . . Could Berlin be Cacciato? I don't really know. The book is actually too complex for me. But I like exploring. [M/FR/F86]

Finally, *Going After Cacciato* refocused discussion on questions about which kinds of writing—factual or fictional, traditional or unconventional—are best able to represent the nature and meaning of the war in Vietnam. Could a work of "fiction" say something "true" about the war? Could a bizarre and fanciful novel like *Cacciato* render an authentic account of the Vietnam experience? Some students were skeptical.

Going After Cacciato . . . is a fiction story about Vietnam. How can you get a feel for the war through writing not based on facts? [F/FR/F86]

But other students disagreed.

Often "fiction" is a better representation of people in a particular place and time than "factual" accounts. [F/JR/S88]

Cacciato is . . . a fiction book. That doesn't mean what's in it is false though. . . . In many ways *Cacciato* is a true story. [M/FR/F86]

And some students claimed that *Cacciato* offered an authentically complex view of the war, a view that, in one student's words, was "full of uncertainty and possibility," a view that, at last, was "as complex as the war was" [F/FR/F86].

The complexity of *Dispatches* and especially *Going After Cacciato* precipitated moments of confusion or consternation for students. Nevertheless, it was those two challenging texts that most clearly prompted a reorientation of students' judgments: away from intensity of response and toward assessments of the authenticity and artistry of the books they were reading. For example, when she reviewed her journal at the end of the semester, one of the freshmen noticed that the center of gravity in her entries had shifted away from affective responses and toward more reflective questions:

After I reread my journal . . . I noticed a subtle progression in the tone of my entries. In the early stages, all of my entries consisted of "I feel sorry for" sentences. Toward the end, I was asking more questions. [F/FR/F86]

By asking questions about issues of authenticity and artistry, many of the students found that they had become "critics," evaluative readers of literary texts.

4 Critical Inquiry

Can one really believe what he reads in his history book? This is an account from one person. Who is this person? What are his credentials? Was he there? If so, did he see what happened or did he talk to people? I never thought about pondering questions like that when reading my history book. [M/FR/F86]

From the outset of the course, I tried to encourage both personal connection and critical reflection, believing not only that the emotional and the rational could provide complementary ways of knowing, but also that a merging of heart and mind would stimulate inquiry.[1] Rosenblatt makes the point that it is easier to think "rationally" about issues when they are presented in an impersonal or abstract way than it is to reflect on those same problems when they are infused with intense feeling or personal significance. What students need to learn, therefore, is not simply how to think critically but how to "think rationally within an emotionally colored context." Or as Rosenblatt puts it succinctly: "Reason should arise in a matrix of feeling" (*Literature as Exploration* 227–28).

The short personal narratives from *Everything We Had* provided such a matrix early in the course: in addition to evoking students' emotional responses, these brief accounts invited reflection on soldiers' experiences. For example, in the selection entitled "Size-Twelve Boot, Size-Ten War," students read about two soldiers who served in Vietnam in 1967 and 1968. Scott Higgins, the compound coordinator at a major headquarters in Bien Hoa (near Saigon), worried about how to hire bar girls for the club, how to scrounge luxuries (such as water heaters) to maintain billets for high-ranking officers, and—occasionally— how to avoid incoming rockets. James Hebron, a sniper and fire-team leader with the Twenty-sixth Marines at Khe Sanh, worried about staying alive on point, coping with inadequate food and equipment (he is provided with size-twelve boots for his size-ten feet), and surviving the physical and psychological trauma of combat.

From these two dramatically different accounts, students began to develop an appreciation for the diversity of soldiers' experiences. Many were incredulous that Higgins could live so well while Hebron suffered so terribly.

As I read the accounts by Scott Higgins and James Hebron, I couldn't believe my eyes. While one man was risking his life day in and day out, the other was worried about hiring bar girls for a hotel. That isn't fair! [F/SR/S88]

Students were disconcerted to learn that, in fact, relatively few soldiers experienced the sustained combat of Hebron's tour, although that experience was the one that many of them had accepted as nearly universal and paradigmatic.

The accounts by Hebron and Higgins also provided one of the earliest opportunities for comparative-critical inquiry. The two soldiers received their assignments under quite different circumstances. Hebron had no choice: he was a Marine Pfc and was destined for a combat assignment. Higgins' story, however, was more complex. After his arrival in Vietnam, Higgins was interviewed and told he could choose between serving with a searchlight platoon or with a convoy escort platoon. Of the first assignment he decided that "as soon as you turn on the light, everybody knows where you are" (88). But the other job didn't appeal to him either. So he convinced the officer in charge of assignments

to find him a different job. As a result Higgins got a safe assignment at Bien Hoa, where his first job was to hire bar girls for the
officers' club. Some students empathized with Higgins' behavior.

I sided with Higgins for wanting a safe assignment no matter
how he got it. I have trouble understanding guys like Hebron
who are so naive and wanted to go fight. [F/FR/F86]

But others were dismayed by his actions.

It really made me sick to read about the corruption that went on
during the war. I usually would look back to see the photographs
and see what the guys looked like, but not with Higgins. I was
disgusted with him. [M/SR/S86]

While these first attempts often lacked sophistication, I tried to
nurture students' early efforts to adopt a critical stance.

As they read more of the stories in Santoli's collection, I encouraged students to examine these intense accounts with a
skeptical eye. Some students were surprised that I wanted them
to take a critical stance.

Now you guys say, "Read critically." I never even considered
that the things I hear aren't one-hundred percent truthful. [F/FR/
F86]

I naturally assumed that each [account] was written with honesty
and sincerity. It never crossed my mind that any Vietnam veteran
would lie or exaggerate about his story to the extent that it would
be unbelievable. [F/JR/S88]

And some balked at the notion that they should evaluate or
judge soldiers' stories.

Who am I to judge actions that I don't really understand, and
especially since I have never been in any kind of similar or even
remotely similar situation. [M/FR/F89]

After reading Higgins' account I had a hard time making a judgment as to whether I thought of his actions as being cowardly in ducking out of the job as searchlight platoon officer or convoy escort platoon officer. I think that perhaps the reason I had a hard time in passing judgment on Higgins is that I felt that I had no right to pass judgment on anyone who had been in Vietnam, since I hadn't been there and could not begin to know what the experience must feel like. [M/SR/S88]

This reluctance to scrutinize soldiers' accounts was not, of course, entirely misguided: the students rightly discerned that they should be cautious when making judgments about a realm of experience far removed from their own. And they were also correct in realizing that soldiers' stories have a certain degree of face validity, a legitimate claim to being "primary" accounts of the experience of war. But such instincts, while not altogether wrong, failed to recognize not only the general limitations of retrospective accounts but also the specific kinds of distortions and discrepancies that pervade most war stories. Through their reading and reflection, students would, I hoped, discover that personal accounts offer some of the best and the worst—the truest and the most distorted—sources of information about what the war was like.

One way that I tried to encourage critical reflection about retrospective accounts was to present some ideas from the psychology of memory, especially theories of memory as a "constructive process." I adapted ideas from several sources, but relied on the accessible account in a popular undergraduate psychology textbook, Philip G. Zimbardo's *Psychology and Life*. In his chapter "Remembering and Forgetting," Zimbardo presents the view that "sometimes what we 'remember' is more than what we actually experienced or different from it in important ways." That is the case because people "construct" memories by fitting new information or perceptions into what they already know: as they process new material into memory, people "frequently add details to make it more complete or change it to make it fit better with other, already existing information in our personal memory store" (328). As Zimbardo points out, by changing information so that it conforms with previous knowledge or beliefs, we are distorting what we remember. Moreover, we are usually "quite unaware of such changes and confidently believe that our 'memory' is an accurate record of what took place" (328).

The lesson is that soldiers' recollections are never simply transcriptions, recordings, or mental photographs of events as they actually occurred. And the implication, of course, is that one must be careful about accepting soldiers' claims and stories, however honest and well-intended, as gospel truth. That idea surprised many students. As one of them wrote:

I guess I hadn't really thought about us filling in those spots in our memory when we can't remember every detail. A lot of the things we remember in everyday life even aren't so factual, even if we repeat them soon after. I question now all the credibility and all those stories I have read and even stories I tell myself. [F/FR/F86]

Most students took seriously the implications of constructive memory, and they tried to apply it as they reflected on both their own experiences and the trustworthiness of the oral histories.

After today's discussion I began to think about how much of what I was reading was the exact truth. In the beginning of my reading, I took it for granted that all of it was true. Now that I think about it, it makes sense these people may remember something other than the true reality. . . . When I first started reading the literature for this class I believed it all. I guess I didn't question their stories as true or false. After today's lecture I began to think about the stories. I read Mock, Beamon, and Lawrence's stories. I began questioning their ability to remember the reality of the war. [F/FR/F86]

Another way in which I tried to provoke students' reflections about the status of personal accounts was to engage them in a discussion of the reasons that soldiers talk about their experiences—or tell their "war stories." To start this discussion, I listed the most obvious reason on the board: "To tell others what the experience was really like." Then I also wrote two statements from an article by a Vietnam veteran, William Broyles, Jr.:

Every good war story is, in a least some of its crucial elements, false.

The better the war story, the less of it is likely to be true. ("Why Men Love War" 61)

As the students quickly pointed out, if these statements about war stories being "false" have any validity, then there is a problem with the claim that personal accounts are primarily intended to tell the truth. Why, then, do soldiers tell stories about their war experiences? There was usually an awkward silence at this point. The students apparently had not thought about people's stories as anything other than accounts of the way things actually were.

But discussion soon led—sometimes by way of talking about more familiar situations, such as the stories people tell about football games, fishing trips, or first dates—to several other reasons that we tell stories about our experiences. For example, people often relate stories as much to entertain their listeners as to inform them, usually by making a story as shocking or suspenseful as possible. Everyone has stretched a tale to make it more enjoyable. Soldiers, too, alter or embellish the details in their stories to create the best effect on the audience. People also tell stories in order to project a certain image of themselves, often as heroes, tough-guys, or saints. War stories often extol the exploits of a heroic figure, usually the teller or one of his comrades, in a way that enhances his stature.

In addition to these familiar motives, people tell stories for more complex and subtle reasons that have little to do with informing, entertaining, or even enhancing one's image. For example, people sometimes tell stories about their experiences in order to understand those events better, telling and retelling the events that led to the football play that failed, or repeating the details of the car accident that should never have happened. Soldiers, too, tell stories—especially to one another—in order to make sense of the events they participated in. Stories are a way of constructing a personal meaning out of complex, confusing, and painful experiences. Finally, people sometimes tell stories to mark the boundaries between insiders (those who understand the story) and outsiders (those who will never fully comprehend). For example, soldiers tend to use military jargon or Vietnam slang (what one of my students referred to as "the 'Nam language") to establish a sense of solidarity with other veterans. Their stories can be cryptic and allusive because they are talking to others who already know the plots and punchlines. In this way, war stories have a social function, inviting those who understand the story to join the group, barring those who cannot comprehend.[2]

Once students recognized that soldiers' stories could serve multiple purposes, it would be easier, I hoped, for them to be critical in their responses to the accounts. Students could, for example, call an account "exaggerated" without claiming that the teller had been deceitful: perhaps those exaggerations were part of a tale that served a purpose other than literal accuracy. Thus I tried to give students a way to critique soldiers' accounts without necessarily criticizing the tellers of those tales. At the same time, I encouraged students to watch for elements in the oral histories that made them suspicious about the statements being made: exaggerations, inconsistencies, contradictions, implausible claims, self-serving interpretations—any obvious signs that the accounts might not be simply accurate renderings of experience.

At the beginning of the course, students tended to focus their critical comments on such criteria as honesty, objectivity, and plausibility, looking for statements that appeared to be believable or for claims that seemed incredible. For example, many students praised Robert Santos's account, "My Men," for its candor, honesty, and freedom from self-serving exaggeration.

Of all the selections from Santoli, "My Men" by Santos really struck me. This guy is very believable to me. His war story doesn't seem at all exaggerated. He doesn't brag one minute and then say he regrets his actions the next. [F/JR/S86]

On the other hand, students tended to criticize some of the more "macho" tales for their implausibility and lack of objectivity. One story that some students found implausible, because of its apparent exaggerations, was the account by a member of the Navy's elite unit, the SEALs.

"The Green-Faced Frogmen" by Mike Beamon has got to be the most incredible story in this book. . . . This is a story . . . that I read with a lot of skepticism. Who is this guy, James Bond? [M/SR/S86]

And for a number of students, Herb Mock's tale of his adventures during the attack on "Fire-Base Burt" was just too exaggerated for belief. Mock tells a tale in which he plays the role of a tough, brash, even reckless warrior—the kind of man who, in the midst of an all-out attack against his firebase, gets into a fistfight with his friend over who will shoot the fifty-caliber machine gun.

It wasn't until yesterday that I realized that the story was so exaggerated. I didn't think about it like that because I was so intrigued with his story. The way he told it with all the action, I couldn't stop and think, "Hey, this could be some serious bullshit in this story!" Maybe I'm just naive. . . . All I know is now I'll be more skeptical. [F/SO/F89]

Nevertheless, although students' instincts told them not to take all of Mock's account at face value, a number of them qualified their judgments: lacking the experience of combat themselves, they felt in no position to make critical judgments.

I guess Mock is trying to seem like a big stud for continuing his game of craps even though he could have been killed. Actually, I think he's stupid. But you can't really judge what other people do unless you've been in their situation. [F/FR/F89]

Despite my best efforts, a number of students persisted in equating the notion of "being critical" with "criticizing," and they were justifiably reluctant to launch a personal attack against individuals who had suffered and sacrificed so much in Vietnam. That ambivalence about criticizing personal accounts was especially evident in students' responses to Navy pilot William Lawrence's story of his years as a POW: students were both greatly impressed and somewhat skeptical—impressed by Lawrence's resourcefulness and fortitude, but skeptical about his claims to have forgiven his captors and his wife, who remarried while he was in captivity. This struggle to be "critical" without "criticizing" is evident in the following excerpts from students' journals, the first from a senior, the second from a freshman.

William Lawrence . . . is all-forgiving, all-understanding. . . . But to me he carries it way too far. I want to grab him by the neck and yell, "Hey, man, it's OK to be human. Show a little anger, show some fear, and show some hate." All of these feelings have to be inside of him. You just can't rationalize everything like that, it just isn't human. . . . I feel wrong criticizing him, though, because this guy went through a hell of a hard time. [M/SR/S88]

When I first started reading Admiral Lawrence's story, "POW," I thought, "Wow, this guy has really got it together!" . . . Then, as the story went on, it seemed too good to be true. *Nobody* could be so calm, cool, and collected in that situation. How could he not feel any anger or resentment for the Vietnamese? . . . He comes across as such a super hero. . . . Maybe I shouldn't be too hard on him, because many things he did were quite admirable. . . . I know I could not endure seven years in a POW camp and come out . . . the way he did. [F/FR/F89]

My aims in this first unit were to encourage critical reflection about stories that most students found emotionally compelling, thereby initiating a process of inquiry that engaged both heart and mind. As I've pointed out already, students sometimes resisted the notion that they should be critical in their reading of soldiers' accounts, and that resistance increased whenever they empathized strongly with the teller or became intensely involved in the story. Nevertheless, many students were able to begin the process of critical inquiry while they read and responded to the oral histories. I tried to nurture that process throughout the course, but it received special emphasis in the unit that focused on factual accounts of past events (or what I sometimes called, rather loosely, "historical" writing). As one of the freshmen recalled in a retrospective essay:

From the beginning of the course we had been required to examine the material closely and read it with skepticism, but [in the unit on history] my skills were put to the test. [F/FR/F89]

During the unit on historical writing, I tried to encourage reflective thinking about a couple of complex questions: How can we know what really happened in the past? And how should we decide what to believe when there are competing accounts of the same event, all of them claiming to be factual? These questions were the focus for a two-week unit in which students read divergent accounts of what occurred when Communist forces occupied the South Vietnamese city of Hué early in 1968. But these questions were also the focus for an introductory exercise in which students encountered two accounts of what happened during an early but significant engagement in the war: the Battle of Ap Bac.[3]

The Ap Bac exercise served a couple of different purposes. One aim was to alert students, at the very beginning of the course, to some of the complexities they would confront later when they read multiple accounts of the same event. But another goal was to identify some of the assumptions about knowledge that students brought into the course, especially their beliefs about the nature of historical knowledge. My interest in students' epistemological assumptions was informed by two models of intellectual development in the college years: the "Perry Scheme"

and the "Reflective Judgment Model."[4] Despite some key differences, both models agree that students enter a world of epistemological complexity when they come to college, a world in which
their assumptions are challenged and, in many cases, their orientations are altered.

In both schemes of intellectual development, students' views
of knowledge evolve through two or three orientations. Early in
their college experience, some students assume that there are
right and wrong answers to questions and clear-cut solutions to
problems; they believe, moreover, that knowledge resides in
authorities and that solutions to complex problems can be ob-
tained by consulting experts (these students are "dualistic absolutists" in Perry's terms or "dogmatists" in the Reflective Judgment model). But few college freshmen are pure absolutists: they
soon discover—if it somehow eluded them in high school—
that there are multiple interpretations, diverse perspectives, and
competing judgments on many important issues. This recognition leads many of them to suspect that one view is just as valid
as any other, since all views are merely opinions anyway (they
become "simple pluralists" or "skeptics"), and they begin to rely
on feelings, intuitions, and emotional commitments to decide
what to believe. Complexity and relativism become the accepted
norms. Later, typically near the end of college, some students
become "disciplined contextual relativists" according to Perry:
they discover alternative frames of reference from which to view
ideas, and so they learn to compare one view with another,
judging both of them according to particular criteria, derived
from a certain set of assumptions.[5] However, in the Reflective
Judgment model students can, at least theoretically, advance
further to become "probabilists": they come to believe that claims
can be tested through a process of rational inquiry, so that some
claims can be affirmed as probable conjectures, or as rationally
warranted approximations to the truth, or as the best and most
reasonable conclusions of those available at a particular time.[6]

These theories of intellectual development in the college years alerted me to the range of orientations that my students might bring to divergent accounts of an historical event. I expected that some students would assume that authorities know the truth about history, and that those students might be dismayed to find more than one authoritative account of an event. Others, convinced of multiplicity and perhaps mired in skepticism, might assume that one can never know what happened in the past, given the fact that observers inevitably see an event from different perspectives and therefore provide different accounts of what happened. Yet other students might make reasoned judgments about the two accounts, deciding that one is more credible than the other on the basis of critical analysis. Thus the developmental models gave me a way to conceptualize my students' responses to discrepant accounts of the same event.

My project was not, however, "developmental" in any strict sense: I did not set out to determine students' positions on a scale of intellectual development, for example.[7] Rather, my aims were more limited and specific: I wanted to find out what kinds of assumptions, orientations, and patterns of deliberation my college students—especially the freshmen—would bring to bear on a situation in which they were faced with conflicting accounts of an event. Therefore, at the beginning of the course I asked them to respond to two reports of what happened at the Battle of Ap Bac, an early engagement between Viet Cong and South Vietnamese troops.

I wrote the two accounts myself, basing them on actual reports and interpretations of the battle. (The full problem is reproduced in appendix A.) The two versions are about the same length, contain the same number of notes, and seem to be based on equally "authoritative" sources. But the accounts paint different pictures of what happened at the battle. In general, Account 1 attempts to put the massive South Vietnamese attack against a small Viet Cong unit in the best possible light, whereas Account 2 tries to portray the South Vietnamese attack as inept and the VC defense as heroic. For example, in the first account the VC are referred to as the "battle-tested 514th Viet Cong Battalion, about five hundred soldiers, including specialists in antiaircraft and antitank tactics"—the writer's obvious attempt to make the Communists appear strong in order to account for the difficulty of the battle and the heavy casualties suffered by the South Vietnamese troops (the ARVN). In Account 2, by contrast, the communists are "two companies of Viet Cong (about two hundred forty soldiers) reinforced with about fifty local guerrillas"— a clear effort to portray the VC as relatively weak, so that their ability to repel the attack will seem heroic.

Although both accounts cite apparently authoritative books about the war, Account 2 includes comments from an American officer who was on the scene,[8] as well as assessments by journalists who are identified as French and Australian[9]—correspondents who might reasonably be expected to be less biased than American or Vietnamese commentators, especially from the military. By contrast, Account 1 cites the optimistic judgments of American and South Vietnamese generals who were not themselves at the battle, as well as the assessment of an American military analyst. To complicate matters, however, Account 1 seems to have a slightly more "objective" tone in much of its recounting of the battle, even though it ends with the comments of the generals. Account 2 sounds almost like a Communist propaganda broadcast in its rendering of the battle; nevertheless, it ends with the American advisor's statement that the South Vietnamese attack was a "miserable damn performance," as well as similar assessments from foreign journalists.

Finally, the first account seems to make more believable claims about the outcome of the battle, whereas the claims in the second account sound exaggerated. For example, the numbers cited in Account 2 seem suspicious: according to this account, the VC unit, outnumbered ten to one and armed with only light weapons, stopped six tanks and inflicted heavy casualties on the ARVN troops, while losing only a few men (three left on the battlefield). In Account 1, on the other hand, the numbers of dead are roughly equal for the two sides, a plausible outcome because the ARVN's superior numbers and firepower are counterbalanced by the VC's choice of position and fortifications.

The first time I taught the course, I talked with students individually, during a conference in my office, about their responses to the two accounts of the Battle of Ap Bac. But in subsequent semesters, when I taught large classes of freshmen, I changed to a written-response format, printing three questions on a single sheet of paper with room for responses:

When historical accounts of the same event are different, can you believe one of the accounts more than another? Why?

Is either of these two acounts more likely to be true? Please explain your answer.

What *really* happened at Ap Bac? Why do you think so?

I want to focus my analysis on the answers that the students in my two freshman courses gave at the beginning of the semester, shortly after they had arrived at college. (I also asked these students to respond to the Ap Bac problem at the end of the course, and I will consider their final responses later.) What I wanted to find out from this exercise was something about my students' orientations to discrepant accounts and their abilities to make reasoned judgments about them.

When the freshmen encountered the two versions of the Battle of Ap Bac, some of them were puzzled and uncertain how to proceed:

I'm sure that one of these would have to be more true, but I don't know which one. I have no idea of exactly what went on there. I really don't know what happened at Ap Bac. I have no idea which account to believe. They both share some important points, but they differ enough to confuse me as to what to believe. I really don't know. [F/FR/F86]

For some, the discrepancies seemed so extensive that they could not imagine how a person could choose one over the other.

When both sides are completely different with their facts, like how many were killed and wounded, it makes it almost impossible to tell. . . . I don't believe that you can honestly tell when both sides are completely opposite in their stories. [F/SO/F86]

Accustomed, no doubt, to reading a single, authoritative history of an event, some students were perplexed to find two accounts of the battle. But others, while equally uncertain about what happened at Ap Bac, were not at all surprised to find different accounts of the same event. One student expressed this view succinctly:

Those accounts are based on someone's point of view and of course they're someone who is different, so that's why you have more than one account. [F/FR/F86]

The conviction that observers' accounts will inevitably differ was fairly common in my freshmen's responses. Perhaps this is a sign of the "multiplicity" that Perry talks about so convincingly: a conception of knowledge in which rival accounts are simply the result of inevitable differences in perspective or point of view.

Everyone views different activities in different ways. One reporter could have seen one aspect of the battle and the other another. It all depends on the individual reporting on the incident. Everyone has different opinions, thus different accounts. . . . Each report is a different view of the battle. Each report comes from what the reporter saw or what he wanted to see. [M/FR/F86]

Some students went even further, claiming that the discrepant reports can be equally valid—different, of course, but equally true. There is thus no basis for comparative evaluation.

I feel they are both true in each of their eyes. I think that both sides are true. [F/FR/F86]

No, you really can't believe one more than the other, simply because they're someone's personal account—of course it's true to them. [F/FR/F89]

To complicate matters further, some students recognized that writers may distort their reports, whether consciously or not, to make them fit with their biases and ideological commitments. This is especially true during war, when officials use propaganda to encourage their followers and discourage the enemy.

> Both of the accounts were biased toward one outlook or the other so some of the truth in what really happened was manipulated and turned around until it suited the writer's need. [M/FR/F89]

Given the pervasiveness of bias and the inevitability of distortion, there may seem to be no warrant for pursuing an inquiry into these two accounts. Did the students give up? Did they refuse to evaluate the accounts? Some of them did: between a quarter (fall 1989) and a third (fall 1986) of the freshmen said they could not make a decision about which account was more likely to be true.[10] (I will return to these "skeptical" students later.) But most of the students, even some who initially said they could not believe one account more than another, were nevertheless willing to propose a basis on which to accept one of the accounts of Ap Bac. More freshmen favored Account 2;[11] however, my interest is not so much in students' decisions as in the reasons they gave for their choices. Those reasons are intriguing because they reveal the bases on which college freshmen were able to accept one of the accounts as true. I want to examine the most salient reasons that students gave for their decisions, illustrating them with excerpts from the responses they wrote during the first week of the course.

A small number of students proposed that the strength of an author's credentials was an important consideration when evaluating rival accounts of the same event. The primary criterion seemed to be whether an author was present as an observer of the event being discussed.

> I would need to know the background of the authors. *If* an author had been there that night then *yes*, I would believe his side. Yes, just because he was there. [F/FR/F86]

Another consideration was the author's objectivity or impartiality.

The author of an account plays an important factor in believing its authenticity. Was it an American, Viet Cong, or an impartial observer who wrote it? [M/FR/F86]

Although evaluating the author's background, biases, and credentials is a good strategy *in general* (and would prove relevant later, in the Hué unit), it is not very helpful in the case of Ap Bac, because there is no indication of who wrote the two accounts of the battle. Hence a more promising approach to evaluating these two accounts involves examining the sources on which they are based. Many students scrutinized the individuals whose views were cited in the two accounts.[12] And most of the students who compared the accounts on the basis of their sources found Account 2 to be superior.

Students gave several reasons that the sources in Account 2 were better than those in Account 1. Their first argument was that because the journalists in Account 2 were not part of the military-political system, they were free to report what they saw, without threat of censorship or fear of adverse consequences.

The second one's sources seem more reliable. One can hardly expect General Harkins and General Cao to admit to a defeat. The colonel and the journalists seem more likely to truthfully examine the battle. [M/FR/F86]

Another, closely related argument was that the two journalists who are cited in Account 2 are French and Australian, and so are probably more neutral than an American would be.

In 1 the only sources are U.S. military, who are likely to show favoritism toward the ARVN, while in 2 sources such as a neutral Australian war correspondent and a French journalist were used. [M/FR/F86]

Third, students tended to be impressed that an American officer, Lieutenant Colonel Vann, would make a negative comment about the performance of the ARVN, the soldiers that the U.S. supported.

> The senior U.S. Army advisor to the ARVN admitted the ARVN attack was "a miserable damn performance." [M/FR/F89]

Finally, students argued that the sources for Account 2—the advisor, certainly, and perhaps the journalists—were present at the battle, whereas the generals cited in Account 1 were far removed from the scene.

> I favor Account 2 because the people interviewed were really at the battle. In Account 1 they were generals who probably got more rosy second-hand information. [M/FR/F86]

In sum, when students analyzed the credibility of the individuals who made claims about the outcome of the battle, they decided that Account 2 had more reliable sources.

Students also argued for the superiority of Account 2 on another basis: its compatibility with things they knew—or believed—about the war.[13] For quite a few students, the strength of the second account comes from its portrayal of the ARVN as ineffective soldiers, a picture of the South Vietnamese that many students accepted as accurate, sometimes because they had heard such claims, sometimes simply because they knew that the South had lost the war. Even at the outset of the course, quite a few students had a negative impression of the ARVN soldiers.

> Based upon the readings I have had before this class, the ARVN troops are known for their clumsiness, noisiness in LPs, and lackadaisical and lighthearted feelings about the war and their efforts. [M/FR/F86]

For these students, the second account of the battle is more consistent with what they know about the behavior of the combatants in the war; hence, that account seems more accurate, and thus more likely to be true. (By the end of the course these impressions were confirmed and strengthened.)

Finally, some students felt that the second version of the battle was "more precise" [M/FR/F86], or "more detailed and specific" [F/FR/F86]—in short, that it was the more factual account.[14]

The second account is more likely to be true. The main reason for this is because all of the counts of wounded and dead are much more precise. In the first account, on the other hand, words such as "about" and "around" are used in explaining the number of casualties. [F/FR/F86]

But while many students decided that features of Account 2— its reliable sources, its realistic portrayal of the capabilities of ARVN and VC forces, its specific and precise details—made it the more credible version of the battle, a number of other students decided, nonetheless, that certain features of Account 1 made it the more believable version of events at Ap Bac. What did Account 1 have that Account 2 didn't?

In many students' eyes, Account 1 had a more restrained and plausible set of claims about the outcome of the conflict. Or perhaps it would be more accurate to say that, in terms of plausibility, the first account won by default: the implausibility of the claims in Account 2 led a number of students to reject that account as a credible version of the battle. Quite a few students agreed that the statistics in Account 2 seem suspicious, and that there is an inconsistency between claims about the relative strength of the two forces and claims about the outcome of the battle.

The first account is easier to believe. The casualties for the VC in the second account are ridiculously low. All of the events, such as the helicopters being destroyed by the machine gun fire, seem vastly exaggerated in the second account. Wouldn't the ARVN be able to kill more than three people while the VC were destroying their helicopters and killing their men? [F/FR/F89]

But there was another factor that led students to view Account 1 as the more believable version: its language, as well as its claims, were more restrained, more "objective." By contrast, Account 2 sounds suspiciously like a communist propaganda broadcast.

The second account seems incredibly biased—the VC do everything right and the ARVN do everything wrong. . . . The VC were like superheroes with their four guns and other meager supplies. [F/FR/F89]

Not all students agreed. Some felt that Account 2 was more "realistic," since it portrayed "our side," the American-advised ARVN, as losers. But for the most part, those students who considered the relative plausibility of the two accounts decided in favor of Account 1, usually because they could not accept the exaggerated claims in the second account.

I believe the first account because it is more probable. The VC having advanced warning of five hundred soldiers is more likely than the VC armed with only four machine guns and rifles against three thousand crack soldiers. Even more improbable was the casualty count. The VC lost only three? . . . I think the first account is more believable, if only because of the statistics involved. I mean, "a squad of fifteen men destroyed four of the tanks and damaged two others." *Really.* In the movies maybe! [F/FR/F86]

In my analysis of these responses to the Ap Bac problem, I have tried to identify the strategies that students used to decide which account (or parts of an account) are closest to what really happened. As I have illustrated, when students were asked to make a decision about the accounts, they tended to base those judgments on such criteria as credibility of sources, consistency with known facts, quality of factual evidence, and plausibility of claims. Thus, while they often lacked sophistication—tending, for example, to rely too heavily on their intuitions about credibility or their impressions of plausibility—the freshmen in my courses were, on the whole, able to judge competing accounts on the basis of one or more appropriate criteria. These findings seem to support the view that college freshmen, far from being mired in dogmatism or paralyzed by skepticism, are able to practice some of the tactics of critical analysis. But how far could they range with those tactics? How would their analytical skills fare in a more complex context?

Having worked on the Ap Bac problem at the beginning of the semester, the students were, I hoped, somewhat better prepared for the kind of problem they encountered about six weeks into the course, during the unit in which they read about two views of events in the city of Hué during Tet 1968, when thousands of people were killed, possibly in a deliberate massacre. The students worked with a set of sources that I carefully selected to present two versions of the massacre.[15] Just as in the Ap Bac problem, neither version of those events was satisfactory in every respect: neither view answered all of the questions about the apparent massacre, and neither was so convincing or so well documented that it could be accepted as unequivocally true— not without further inquiry.

Even certain key facts of the massacre are disputed. Because many bodies had been buried in mass graves, sometimes outside Hué in remote jungle areas, the details of the nature and scope of the killing unfolded slowly, over a period of more than a year, and thus claims about the number of bodies found in the graves varied widely. Moreover, there were conflicting reports about the identity of many of the victims found in the graves. Some sources suggest that most of the dead were civilians, and that they were found with hands bound, shot in the head or clubbed to death—or even buried alive. Other sources claim that some of the dead were uniformed soldiers, that many were casualties of the fierce fighting, and that others were victims of the massive air strikes around Hué.

If the facts are disputed, so are the interpretations of what happened and why. One major interpretation, the "massacre" view, claims that the Communists planned to execute government officials, including many minor functionaries, as well as religious leaders and most foreigners. Some sources suggest that the massacre extended even further, including many civilians with only the most superficial connections to the Saigon government. One piece of evidence for this interpretation is the mass graves, which, on this view, contained thousands of civilians who were bound and bludgeoned to death. Another kind of evidence comes from Communist radio broadcasts and captured documents, which appear to confirm the mass killings. And a major source is the testimony of survivors of the occupation, with their poignant stories of relatives killed or taken away by the Communists.

According to a second interpretation, official reports of a massacre were a self-serving myth, concocted on the basis of flimsy evidence, distorted facts, and outright lies. For example, Noam Chomsky and Edward S. Herman[16] claim that the Communists planned to execute only a handful of government officials, slating many more for reeducation and "attempting to rally large numbers with minimal reprisals" (28). Many of the dead and missing civilians could be attributed to the ruthlessness of the U.S. counterattack against Hué, during which U.S. forces used their massive firepower indiscriminately and with devastating effects. Proponents of this view cite evidence that contradicts the "massacre" version of events: they state, for example, that bodies in some of the graves wore uniforms, suggesting that some of the dead were soldiers killed in battle; they claim that on at least one occasion, a U.S. soldier saw track marks at a grave site, indicating that heavy equipment, which only the U.S. possessed, had been used to dig the graves; and they assert that the official count of bodies was routinely inflated above the numbers reported by more reliable eyewitnesses. But many of the arguments of the "myth" proponents are designed to discredit elements of the "massacre" view.

The "myth" proponents present three main reasons to doubt

the "massacre" version of events in Hué. First, they claim that the source for all official accounts of the massacre, accounts which were released to the American press and published in most newspapers and magazines, was the story created by the South Vietnamese Army's Tenth Political Warfare Battalion in Saigon, a unit whose mission was to manufacture propaganda that would discredit the Communists. The Political Warfare Battalion was therefore hardly an unbiased or reliable source. Second, myth proponents claim that the captured documents in which the North Vietnamese supposedly planned a large-scale massacre were deliberately mistranslated. Third, myth proponents point out that the story of the massacre became important only a year later, in March 1969, when officials were embarrassed by revelations of U.S. involvement in a massacre at My Lai. At this same time, President Nixon, struggling to find a justification for prolonging the war, argued that American soldiers had to continue to fight because a "bloodbath"—like the one in Hué— would occur if American troops withdrew too hastily, leaving the South Vietnamese to face the Communists' reprisals. Thus there were political motives for concocting a tale of massacre.

Despite these problems with the "massacre" account, there are several reports of widespread killing that cannot be easily dismissed. Some of these reports are from individuals who were in Vietnam during the period of the massacre and who went to Hué then or later to talk with people about what happened. For example, Don Oberdorfer, a reporter for the *Washington Post*, based the account in his book *Tet!* on observations during the battle as well as later visits to Hué. His stories of the terror and suffering in Hué are gripping and compelling. Following his investigations, Oberdorfer concluded that there were "2800 victims of the occupation, shot to death, bludgeoned or buried alive in the most extensive political slaughter of the war" (201).

Other reports of the massacre come from foreign journalists or service volunteers, individuals who seem to be relatively free from bias. A moving account of the suffering in Hué can be found in Alje Vennema's book, *The Vietcong Massacre at Hué*. A Canadian doctor who worked as a volunteer at a provincial hospital in South Vietnam, Vennema says he was opposed to U.S. involvement in Vietnam, and that he initially doubted reports of a Communist massacre at Hué. But when he went to Hué to investigate, he found considerable evidence that many civilians were led out of Hué, murdered by the Communists, and buried in mass graves. Yet another individual who opposed U.S. policy in Vietnam, British journalist Stewart Harris, wrote that he had seen evidence from graves around Hué that convinced him that the Communists had executed many Vietnamese and some foreigners. Harris says: "I am sure of this after spending several days in Hué investigating allegations of killing and torture. I saw and photographed a lot for myself, but inevitably I relied on many civilians and soldiers. . . . All seemed honest witnesses" (36).

In short, during the two-week unit on the Hué Massacre, students were faced with a more complex version of the Ap Bac problem: they were asked to inquire into an event for which there are disputed facts, discrepant claims, and rival interpretations. And their assignment was to write a paper in which they made a case for what really happened in Hué, taking account of all relevant evidence and arguments.

I assumed that their previous encounter with discrepant accounts would ease some of the impact of the Hué problem, the shock of finding that authorities disagree, that even "history" entails conjectures and refutations, rather than certainties. And that experience with Ap Bac probably did prepare many of the students for the unit on Hué. But what stood out in the journal entries were the reactions of those students who were distressed by the contradictory claims about what happened at Hué.

Well, I'm about to have a heart attack! You guys scare me to death sometimes! I just read the articles on Hué (at least the first few) and I can't believe how contradictory they are. . . . I don't know, really know how to approach these articles. I mean, I wasn't there, I really don't have any idea what truly happened, yet how will I EVER know? I won't! I may get a basic idea, but I'm never really going to know for sure. . . . How am I going to know what to believe?? [F/FR/F86]

As I read these articles, I find myself really confused about what happened at Hué. Each article has a different version of what happened. How do I know what to believe? . . . The worst part for me is not knowing if they are true or if they are right or wrong. [F/FR/F89]

And for some students, the claims about the massacre were so contradictory that it seemed unlikely that anyone could determine what really happened.

In reading the assignment for today I found myself very confused. A couple of the people writing the articles kept telling us something and then saying why or how it was untrue. By the time I was done with those articles, I didn't have any idea what to believe. [F/FR/F86]

I was particularly intrigued by those statements that suggested confusion, uncertainty, and skepticism, signs that students' assumptions were being challenged. And I tried to respond in ways that would be sympathetic and encouraging. For example, when a student's journal entry revealed anxiety about her confusion, I tried to endorse uncertainty as a valuable component of inquiry. The student, a junior in one of my small courses, wrote that the Hué readings had her "pretty confused":

I really wonder if anyone can really know the truth about things that have happened in the past. . . . Sometimes just living in the present is difficult, and now I must analyze and determine what actually happened several years ago. Is that possible? I'm sure that with the guidance of Professor Kroll everything will become clear, but until then, I don't know, I'm still apprehensive. [F/JR/S86]

Here is what I wrote in the margin of her journal:

97

Don't count on him too much. He's still confused a lot too. Basically, I hope you can accept "intelligent confusion" as healthier than "ignorant certainty." There's a time to tolerate ambiguity and put up with uncertainty, while you're sifting through accounts and looking at different views. Then there's a time to make some decisions and judgments—based on the best evidence you have: maybe not absolute certainty or the truth for all time, but what looks very probable given what you know.

In short, I empathized with students when they felt confused or perplexed, but I also tried to elicit critical inquiry through the comments I made in the journals. I tried to encourage students' best efforts to articulate alternative positions, to determine which facts supported which interpretations, and to subject all sources, claims, and evidence to critical scrutiny. In fact, much of my "teaching" about critical thinking took place either in the comments I wrote in the journals or in my responses to class discussions. What I sought to avoid was lecturing directly about the massacre, because I did not want to endorse one position or another. The only lecture that I—or, in the freshman courses, one of my assistants—typically gave was an orientation to critical inquiry: an introduction to the idea that we were going to read "factual" (or "historical") accounts with a critical eye. One of the freshmen recorded her impressions of this lecture in a journal entry:

Today in lecture one of the associate instructors talked about . . . biases and how we should be skeptical of history. We discussed how to look for the credibility of the author and to distinguish facts from opinions. It was really strange to learn to read that way, because all through elementary school, junior high, and high school we were always taught to memorize history. We never even thought about questioning the text. All we did was spit out the facts and we got all the points. We never had to interpret anything. That is really scary, because so many things go into the writing of history. Different things get edited out, and different things are stressed more in every different history book. I guess I just always thought that my history books were 100 percent true and unbiased, but I've realized that that is virtually impossible. . . . It's really weird because you think you can read and memorize and have all the facts, but what you know can be very far from the actual truth. [F/FR/F89]

After the initial shock wore off, most of the students began to make many of the same kinds of judgments about the accounts of the Hué Massacre as they had made about the two versions of Ap Bac: they evaluated the trustworthiness of the authors and their sources, they assessed the cogency of factual evidence, and they analyzed the plausibility of claims and rival interpretations. For example, when they examined the trustworthiness of the authors and their sources of information, students tended to be skeptical about those accounts that came from governmental agencies.

You must always (and I mean *always*) look carefully at anything the government and/or military puts out as the "truth." Not saying that it's always wrong, but it may be slightly altered to get the picture they want. [F/FR/F86]

Other students, while generally suspicious of authors and their sources, recognized that a judgment about events in Hué would nonetheless have to be based on the available accounts. The task, then, was to decide which articles were *relatively* reliable.

When I read the first few accounts in the packet I thought that I would never be able to figure out what really happened at Hué. . . . Slowly, I did learn that there were certain things you could look for in the articles to help you decide if you should believe the information or not. One . . . is the author's point of view, where they were when the event happened. . . . Another thing to look at in the author is their authority and reliability. . . . The last really important thing I learned to examine is the author's motives for writing the article in the first place; what are his interests and concerns? . . . If you can figure this out, then you'll most likely have the best evidence to base your decisions on. [F/FR/F89]

Many students tended to accept as reasonably accurate accounts from those individuals who went to Hué to investigate the massacre for themselves.

One important factor in [the *Time*] article is that the reporter *was there*. He had seen it for himself. Also, he opposed U.S. policy in Vietnam, so why would he lie? If he says that there were many political leaders . . . who were murdered and buried in mass graves, what does he have to gain? This does not make his article automatically true, though. I think it makes it *more* believable. [M/FR/F89]

For a number of students, it was important that Dr. Vennema, author of one of the major accounts of the massacre, was not an American, and that he claimed to be opposed to the war in Vietnam.

I feel there is more just reason to believe someone like Dr. Vennema. Being a Canadian he had less of a bias than someone from the United States or Vietnam. [F/FR/F89]

Similarly, most students were inclined to believe reports from British journalist Stewart Harris (*London Times*) and journalist Don Oberdorfer (*The Washington Post*).

Oberdorfer's story includes many specific interviews and events. . . . The *London Times* reporter says he is "quite sure" about what happened, and his sources appear to be reliable. All in all, these accounts are pretty convincing. [M/SR/S86]

Although such considerations as the trustworthiness of authors and their sources were important for many students, others tended to focus on the claims in the various articles, attempting to assess their plausibility and basis in evidence. In the following excerpt, for example, we can see a freshman scrutinizing a point in Chomsky and Herman's article.

In another example, a photographer, David Douglas Duncan, said that "in the smashed ruins lay two thousand dead civilians."

The authors claimed that this number was higher than any estimates of killing by VC. Even so, Duncan never mentioned that these civilians were killed by American soldiers; Chomsky and Herman just assumed that they were. Also, a Canadian doctor, in the grave sites he examined, found only 68 bodies instead of the officially claimed 477. But that does not mean that he examined all the graves. Even though the authors proved that the U.S. was using propaganda, they were not very convincing in attempting to show that the Americans were more brutal than the Viet Cong and that they killed more civilians. [M/FR/F89]

When students engaged in this kind of critical reflection in their journals, I made supportive comments in the margins. Many of these comments were brief words of encouragement, variations on "good point here," "well put," "good observation." But when students' entries were less critically reflective, I urged them to base their thinking on evidence or to probe more deeply into the claims and arguments about the massacre. Here are examples of the comments that I wrote in response to statements in three students' journals.

STUDENT: In other words, the brutal and senseless murders at Hué were not due to overeager soldiers who had become programmed to kill, rather they were highly organized executions.
COMMENT: OK—but look for strong evidence for this view.
STUDENT: It's hard to figure out which side is right, but I'm inclined to believe the official reports that thousands of people were found in mass graves and victims of the Communists.
COMMENT: Why? You need to base this on more than intuition or prejudice. Is the evidence somewhat stronger?
STUDENT: What about the rest of the bodies? I would surmise most of those were of civilians who were killed in the allied retaking of Hué.
COMMENT: Is there any evidence to support this? Look for it.

I hoped that students would begin to imitate these kinds of questions, raising them as part of their own critical inquiry. In at least some cases, I saw it happen. As a senior wrote in his final essay:

In my analysis of the Hué Massacre, I read different stories by different sources, and many were in conflict. Now when I read something, I can envison Dr. Kroll reminding me: "Ask yourself why this was written." [M/SR/S88]

For some students, the most salient point about the "massacre" was neither the discrepant claims nor the diverse interpretations, but rather the brute fact that a large number of innocent people were killed.

It doesn't matter who won the battle of Hué. It matters, though, that innocent people suffered. . . . Many people died at Hué. Maybe we need to think about the people instead of who did [what] or who to blame. [F/FR/F89]

And for those students who were profoundly disturbed by the bloodshed, it seemed more important to sympathize with the suffering in Hué than to deliberate over who was responsible for how many deaths.

I am not too thrilled with this next assignment, it's so academic: "Was there a massacre at Hué?" . . . an academic debate. I have read a few of these accounts. . . . Who's right? Somebody died— I can just see myself, standing on a hill above the carnage. The sky is burnt red, as billows of grey-green smoke float across the background. Rubble and jagged concrete are strewn among dusty, bloody bodies . . . arms and legs recklessly twisted. People died. Is it a question of how many? Does it make it more important if three thousand were brutally murdered or three? [F/FR/F86]

The Hué problem clearly asked these students to "think rationally within an emotionally colored context" (to use Rosenblatt's phrase once more). I tried to comment on their journal entries in a way that would encourage reflection but without discouraging heartfelt response. For example, when a student wrote that "reading information on the Hué Massacre literally makes me sick," I replied:

Critical Inquiry

I'm glad you see the human tragedy—that can't be overlooked (though it sometimes get ignored, I'm afraid). Still, I hope you can see another approach to the Hué incident: that it poses a problem of understanding and judgment. It seems to me that a person can respond both emotionally and intellectually to this event, and perhaps that either response by itself is going to be partial and incomplete.

In sum, I urged students to come to the most reasonable decision they could about events in Hué during the 1968 Tet Offensive, so that they could write a paper that made a plausible case for what really happened. For most students, a thoughtful decision seemed possible, if difficult.

It's not an easy thing to accomplish, but with careful analysis, time, and some knowledge or background of what happened, you can come to your own conclusion of what to believe. It's important to keep an open mind and study more than one view or account. [F/FR/F86]

By comparing claims, sources, and evidence, most of the students were able to arrive at a reasoned judgment about what probably happened in Hué.

It's not so much that I am absolutely sure what went on—I don't believe that's possible. But I think a careful comparison of the sources, taking any possible biases into account, should be able to lead us to a reasonable assumption of what really took place. [M/SR/S86]

And despite the struggle, most of them were proud of what they had accomplished. A junior expressed those feelings especially well in her retrospective essay:

My first battle was Hué. I was bombarded with page after page of conflicting historical information. I was confused and frustrated. There were so many accounts of Hué. How can all of them be right? How can all of them be wrong? . . . For seven nights and eight days I pored over the Hué literature (the nights were especially bad). Each day I became more skeptical, less gullible.

103

I felt myself become stronger, more critical. In the end I mastered the material, I drew my own conclusions, and ended my Hué experience with a twelve-page masterpiece (if I do say so myself). [F/JR/S86]

When they looked back on the course at the end of the semester, quite a few students mentioned the unit on the Hué Massacre as a significant experience, claiming that it encouraged them to ask tough questions about their knowledge of past events. For some students, "history" became more complicated and problematic.

From looking at the many different views on the accounts at Hué I learned a very important lesson. I had always assumed that . . . in a history book or even an important magazine that the material was totally factual. I soon found out that one cannot get a full perception of what truly happens in any given situation by just reading one article. [F/FR/F86]

But did students really become more critical about alternative accounts of the same historical event? Although I cannot give a conclusive answer to that question, I would like to consider several kinds of evidence that their work on the Hué unit affected students' orientations to critical inquiry.

One piece of evidence comes from a comparison I made of my freshmen's responses to the Ap Bac exercise at the beginning and end of fall semester 1986.[17] For that project, I examined the kinds of reasons students gave for choosing one of the accounts (trustworthiness of sources, plausibility of claims and quality of facts, and consistency with prior knowledge) and I identified the "conceptual orientation" (dogmatic, perspectivist, intuitive, or analytical) that seemed to lie behind those reasons. I also made special note of instances of a "skeptical" orientation: the view that it wasn't possible to choose one account over the other.

One of the most intriguing discoveries was a marked shift in the kinds of "skeptical" statements that students made at the beginning and end of the course.[18] At the beginning, students tended to say that they couldn't choose one account over the other because each version simply represented a different (and equally legitimate) point of view on the same situation. By the end of the semester, however, the skeptical statements tended to reflect a more sophisticated recognition of the limitations of historical knowledge and the difficulties of making judgments on the basis of only two accounts. In some cases, the same students made differents kinds of skeptical responses at the beginning and end of the course. For example, one freshman wrote at the outset that "it seems the accounts differ because of perspective and what each person wanted to see or thought they saw." But at the end of the course, while he is still concerned about people's biased perspectives, this student is also more reflective about problems of historical judgment:

After reading all the material on Hué, I see now how and why it is so difficult to tell what really happened. I think a lot has to do with what each individual wants to believe. If you want to believe your country is always right, then not much is going to change it. I also think you have to take into account who the sources are and what each has to gain by writing the account. [F/FR/F89]

When I examined the reasons that students gave for choosing one account over the other, I found that they made about the same kinds of statements, with roughly the same frequency, at the end of course as they had at the beginning. But students' justifications for their choices tended to be somewhat more so- phisticated: ratings of the level of "conceptual orientation" re- flected in students' responses were slightly higher at the end of the semester.[19] Moreover, several students said that even though their second responses might appear to be similar to their initial comments, those final answers resulted from better informed or more complex thinking. Here are some comments from students' comparisons of their responses.

Wow! Deja vu. I wrote almost the exact same responses both times. However, now my reasons are more definite and I can support them from reading something like the reports on Hué. [F/FR/F89]

I just compared my responses to the problems you gave us at the beginning of the course. Wow! I cannot believe how similar my solutions were. I mean, they were almost identical. "Well," I thought to my astonished, confused self, "I just went full circle!" . . . I learned and absorbed all the different facts about the war and came up with the same conclusion. Except this time I had all that information to back me up. [F/FR/F86]

In addition, when I asked students whether anything in the course had affected their thinking, many of them claimed, often quite emphatically, to have become more critical readers.

I am critical of almost everything I read and see. I'm always trying to figure out what's being "hidden" in news reports or articles. . . . I am doubtful and suspicious. . . . Anyway, yes, this course has affected me. I'm a critical reader now—where I think I was a little gullible before. [F/FR/F86]

Moreover, a substantial percentage of the students (48 percent in my first freshman course, 41 percent in the second) attributed their critical orientations specifically to their work on the Hué Massacre. The following statements are representative of those responses:

The unit on the Hué Massacre. . . . Now I tend to look at accounts of historical events with a skeptical eye. I can't seem to believe half of what I read anymore. [F/FR/F86]

I think that when we studied about Hué . . . I learned to be more curious and suspicious about historical accounts. I was forced to question the authenticity of a writer. Before I believed anything that was written. Now I'm more cautious. [F/FR/F86]

The readings and writing the paper on what really happened at the Hué Massacre had a strong influence on how I look at accounts of historical events. I realized that when reading conflicting accounts one has to be extremely skeptical of almost everything the author writes. [F/FR/F86]

The Hué paper made me start thinking about historical *truth* rather than historical *facts*. Now when I read a document, questions fill my mind—who is the author, why is he interested in this, are there other documents that disagree with this one? . . . Needless to say this course has opened my eyes and frustrated my mind. [F/FR/F86]

Thus, when students compared their two responses to Ap Bac, they claimed that the course had had an impact on their thinking about accounts of past events, and an impressive number of them mentioned the unit on the Hué Massacre as a primary influence. Although undergraduates might be unreliable judges of such influences, their self-assessments seem to be careful and thoughtful. Also, when I examined entire portfolios of materials (Ap Bac responses, self-analyses, journal entries, retrospective essays), I discovered quite a few cases in which the course seemed quite clearly to have provided significant opportunities for critical inquiry. Let me focus once again on Karen, the freshman whose responses I've considered in previous chapters.

Karen provides a fairly typical example of the ways that many of the freshmen struggled with critical inquiry. At the beginning of the semester, she had a thoughtful response to the Ap Bac exercise, agreeing with the majority of her classmates that Account 2 is "more likely to be true." Karen justified her choice by saying that the sources for that account seem more "impartial and unbiased" (she cites the French and Australian journalists) and that the second account contains "more specific data and details." At the end of the course, she again chose Account 2 as more likely to be true, and for nearly the same reasons. But between those two responses lay a serious and substantial effort to engage in critical inquiry.

During the first weeks of the course, Karen was encouraged to take a critical stance toward the personal narratives in *Everything We Had*. Like many of her peers, Karen was drawn into the soldiers' experiences, empathizing with their trials and sorrows, perhaps because her father had been a soldier in Vietnam. And because she felt so connected with the soldiers' experience, Karen had to remind herself that she was supposed to be reading the accounts with a critical eye:

I know I need to keep reminding myself to be skeptical, to understand that not every detail in each account is the absolute truth.

That same strategy of critical scrutiny was encouraged during the unit on the Hué Massacre, when students were asked to assess two different explanations of the same event. At the beginning of the semester, Karen seemed to take the Ap Bac exercise in stride, giving a full account of how she would decide which account was more likely to be true. She explained that "I have had experience in the past in examining reports for their credibility and believability." Therefore, she approached the first articles with considerable confidence.

After reading the first two articles in the packet, I already have formed a view or belief. To be honest, after reading Hosmer I thought that was an accurate, believable account of Hué; however, after reading Chomsky and Herman I found the first article sensationalized and not all that accurate. The flaws presented completely discredited Hosmer's document.

Karen decided that Chomsky and Herman had won the debate with Hosmer, just as Account 2 won out in the Ap Bac exercise. But when she read additional material on the Hué Massacre, Karen discovered that the arguments are more complex than those in a debate, so that she would have to struggle to justify a conclusion about what really happened. In short, Karen's confident response to Ap Bac (as well as her initial judgment of the two opposing views of Hué) is somewhat misleading: she did not fully reckon with the epistemological implications of discrepant versions of the truth, as the following journal entry illustrates.

It had previously been hard for me to comprehend the possibility of having two accounts of the same event be completely different.

I did understand the very real possibility of there being inconsistencies, but completely different is another thing. When I think back to the two accounts we read about Ap Bac that were almost opposite, I guess I just assumed one was fabricated. I wasn't sure which, but in my mind there was no way two honest, real accounts could be so different. Now, however, I have a better understanding of how two different accounts can generate from the same event in the Vietnam War.

Although Karen still yearned for certainty, for "real facts" and the "real truth" about the massacre, she persisted in scrutinizing authors' claims, adopting an attitude of critical skepticism. These complex attitudes are evident in a later journal entry, which began with a statement of escalating doubt.

It was very easy for me to accept what an author said happened in Vietnam as fact, as the absolute truth, because I wasn't there and he was. This unit has taught me that even those who were there do not agree, and the possibility exists that some would even purposely fabricate details. . . . Skepticism has become a rule for me now.

Although she had learned to doubt authorities' claims, this skepticism was not very satisfying because it didn't seem to bring her any closer to a decision about what happened in Hué. Skepticism simply breeds more doubts. In a revealing entry made a week later, Karen reflected on her increasing skepticism:

Although I was somewhat skeptical as I read previous to this [Hué] unit, I am much more skeptical now after seeing how "facts" can be twisted. . . . To put it simply, this unit has been a struggle for me. . . . It is tiring and unsettling to think of all the possibilities, explanations, and uncertainties that surround Hué.

Or as she put it in an earlier entry: "What truly frustrates me is that both sides . . . have at least some pieces of evidence in their favor." Despite her frustration, Karen persisted in examining the claims made by the "massacre" and "no massacre" advocates.

The articles that represented this view that there was "no massacre" seemed to have been researched thoroughly to find all of these picky little details (flaws) that all add up to discredit the "massacre" theory or myth. This aspect of the meticulousness with details adds credibility—makes the reader think that someone investigated for a long time and investigated so thoroughly to point out these details. Furthermore, what I think gives more credibility to the "no massacre" theory is that they addressed the opposing view in many of the articles, admitting that the Communists did execute some (most likely) maybe even black-listed some, but that was not the reason for the majority of the deaths. The articles that were "pro massacre" did not address the issues or the opposing possibility.

Later entries reveal the same struggle to balance doubt (edging toward despair) and critical judgment (leading toward a reasonable, if not absolutely certain, conclusion). In one of those entries, Karen began by expressing her frustration and voicing her doubts:

This has been a difficult unit for me. It is confusing and quite frustrating. No matter what one might believe happened at Hué, there exists substantial arguments and evidence against that belief. . . . Then there is the problem with validity and credibility of the evidence, of sources. Maybe there was a massacre, but what about those mistranslations of the captured Vietnamese documents? Then again, how do we know the documents are even valid and someone did not tamper with them to begin with? Or maybe the document was valid and the original translations were correct?

Despite feelings of frustration, however, Karen was able to turn her skepticism toward critical inquiry: toward scrutiny of sources, claims, and evidence. As we see in the next part of her journal entry, Karen could—with encouragement—work toward a decision.

The possibilities are endless, but as Mr. Kroll said, that doesn't excuse us from trying to decipher, if only for ourselves, what happened, based on the evidence given to us. For me, it is hard not to believe a personal eyewitness account (as the ones in Oberdorfer), but I do not believe ten eyewitness accounts of actions which seem to indicate deliberate political killings by the Communists make a massacre.

She concluded this entry with a reflection on the uses of skepticism and the limits of certainty.

All of this skepticism, which is good, I know and believe, makes it extremely challenging for one to determine what it is that he or she truly thinks happened at Hué. And yet, even when that person finally has established a picture in his or her mind, the questions, doubts, and valid opposing arguments still linger.

Karen clearly wrestled with the central problem of critical inquiry: how to reach a probable and rationally justified conclusion when the "truth" cannot be known with certainty. The paper that Karen wrote at the end of the unit reflected her ability to evaluate evidence, her willingness to reach a decision on the basis of analysis, and also her humility in the face of complexity. A couple of sentences from the introduction to her paper give a sense of the style and substance of her argument.

The public was led by the Saigon and United States governments and the press to believe that the Communists, while in control of Hué, engaged in the widespread and unmerciful killings of thousands of Vietnamese. However, the weight of the evidence seems to contradict this theory, and although the Communists did kill select individuals, this number was probably small. A larger number of deaths resulted from the brutal warfare between the U.S. and the Viet Cong.

At the end of the course, Karen responded a second time to the Ap Bac exercise. There are some subtle differences, but in both cases she chose Account 2 as more believable, arguing that the sources for that account are more credible. When she compared her answers from the beginning and end of the course, Karen said that her responses were "essentially the same."

I felt both in the beginning of the course and at the end of the course that the use of neutral sources in a report certainly contributed to its believability.

Nevertheless, her comments also reveal how much she has learned about critical inquiry.

This course and what I learned during the Hué unit taught me to look at more than just whether or not neutral sources were used, which was essentially the only reason I gave at the beginning of the course. I learned to look more closely at the language of the report also. . . . to look at the statistics actually given in the account and check to see if they really add up correctly. In other words, I learned through this course to more fully and completely examine an historical account—its content and its language. This new knowledge still confirmed my view that one historical account can, indeed, seem more believable than another, more likely to be true, more reliable.

Karen's case illustrates the way critical inquiry worked for many of the students in my courses: not by transforming their epistemological orientations, but rather by encouraging habits of analysis and critical reflection. In particular, the Ap Bac exercise and the unit on the Hué Massacre gave students opportunities to engage in active inquiry: a chance to exercise and extend their powers of comparative, interrogative, and evaluative thinking.[20] As students wrestled with conficting accounts and contradictory interpretations, I tried to foster both a propensity to doubt and a willingness to decide: a dialectic between reflective skepticism and reflective judgment. When students rushed toward a decision, I encouraged all their doubts; when they became mired in uncertainty, I insisted on a well-reasoned verdict—trying always to guide them away from either a certainty so strong or a skepticism so severe that they closed their minds to further inquiry.

5 Ethical Inquiry

> I still feel that there are several legitimate views of moral questions, and that any individual can never have an absolute certainty that his or her views are the right ones. However, through careful thought and argument, one can find truths which are at least more defendable than others. [M/JR/S86]

In a guerrilla war like Vietnam, where it was difficult to distinguish friend from foe, stories of soldiers killing civilians (usually "suspected" VC) are commonplace. These acts of killing—some tragic, some deplorable—were depicted in several of the books that students read during the course.

When a Vietnamese housemaid steals a piece of chewing gum from among his possessions, an angry soldier shoots her at point blank range. ("Chrome Dome," *Everything We Had*)

Enraged and frustrated over watching their comrades killed by VC mines, a group of soldiers goes into a village on an unauthorized "snatch" mission, searching for two Vietnamese men whom an informant has identified as VC—although the two had been cleared by official interrogators. The soldiers kill one suspect on the spot, capture the informant by mistake, and kill him on the way back to the base, claiming that he tried to escape. (*A Rumor of War*)

Two well-liked Marines disappear while their unit is on patrol. Some of their comrades later find their bodies in shallow graves in a nearby village, where they also find an old man and a young woman. Although the two Vietnamese claim that they had nothing to do with the killings, they are the only suspects, so the squad executes them in retaliation for their friends' deaths. (*Fields of Fire*)

While on a night ambush, a platoon detects what they assume to be VC guerrillas in and around a hut. Although in the rain and darkness they can't tell for sure who is in the hut, the unit opens fire on the figures. When they go to inspect, the soldiers find dead and dying children everywhere. (*Born on the Fourth of July*)

When is killing justified? Are soldiers responsible for their actions during combat? Do ethical considerations make any sense in a situation where the only law seems to be "kill or be killed"? Is war beyond both rational understanding and moral judgment? I wanted students to begin to ponder such difficult questions. And by reading the literature of the war, I hoped they would explore some of the moral dilemmas that American soldiers confronted in Vietnam.

To initiate their thinking about ethical issues, I asked students during the first week of the course to consider a hypothetical situation, a story that I wrote called "The Rifleman's Dilemma" (see Appendix B).[1] In this story, a soldier named Johnson is stationed on a hilltop while the rest of his squad patrols along a trail that leads to a village in the valley. As he watches, Johnson sees a Vietnamese woman walk onto the trail, bend over, and then move into the brush, just out of sight of the squad but still visible to Johnson. Johnson is suspicious but uncertain. The woman might simply be an innocent peasant, hiding from soldiers whom she fears. But then she might be a member of the local guerrilla forces—who control the area—and she could be preparing to detonate a mine. The squad is about to pass by the woman. They are too far away for Johnson to call out to them, and even a warning shot is unlikely to stop them. Johnson wonders what he should do. As he raises his rifle, he realizes that if he shoots the woman and she is just a peasant, he will have

114

murdered an innocent person; but if he doesn't shoot her and she detonates a mine, he will have allowed her to blow his friends to bits. What should Johnson do—hold his fire or shoot the woman?[2]

The first time I used the Rifleman's Dilemma (spring 1986), I talked individually with students about their reactions, probing their responses to see if I could discover their views about the morality of killing during war. The results were intriguing. Consider the transcript of part of my conversation with Sarah, a junior.

That one was really hard and I had to look at it—it's hard on paper especially because it's so hard to say what you would do. And I guess, though, I think, if it was me, I probably would have shot her because—of my friends. And I would have just had to think, well, sometimes you have to—you know it's really hard to make those decisions—but you have to weigh a life against another life. And I would have felt terrible if it had been the wrong decision, but that's probably what I would have done.

Why does the fact that these people are your friends make a difference?
Because I'm selfish. Because you know this could be somebody else's mother, but at the same time I guess you've got to go with what's important to you and it would make a difference to me.

What if this soldier decides to shoot the woman and it turns out she was just an innocent peasant, caught in a bad set of circumstances, and she's dead. Do you think he's done anything morally wrong?
Well, I know if it was me I'd feel really bad, so I guess when you feel bad it's sort of like you're breaking some sort of morals. But at the same time I think I would justify it by saying I'm in a war and I have to—so I guess—no, if the morals of war are OK. And if they're not OK then you're—but, if that's what you're going on, if that's your basis for morals.

What do you think the morals of war are?
Well, you have to be willing to make judgments like this and maybe be wrong. And that's saying that I guess that you don't always have time to think things over, so you have to, I mean, the morals of war are, if you protect your side and do what, you

know, and try to keep it as good as you can for your side. And try not to worry too much about the other side.

If this guy did it, would you be willing to call him a murderer?
No, because I really believe that any situation, that there's no act that is inherently right or wrong, it's the reasons. I mean, you know, I think that if you look at the situation and you really do what you think is best, then really you've done all you can do. And I'm sure he would regret it, and it probably would make him do a lot of thinking about things, and maybe next time he wouldn't shoot but then maybe next time it would be a booby trap, you know. And I really think that probably he would have felt a lot worse if he had let all his friends die. And it probably would have been—well, I don't really think it would have been more right or really more wrong, but it just would have been what he would have had to deal with. And I know I couldn't deal with the idea that I just choked and I couldn't decide and therefore I let a whole bunch of people die rather than one.

Like many of the responses to the dilemma, Sarah's reactions are complex, evincing several attitudes and ethical orientations. In her first statement, Sarah acknowledges that this dilemma is "hard"—difficult not only because of the unhappy circumstances the rifleman finds himself in, but also because Sarah has to decide what to do "on paper," removed from the actual context of judgment. Although the problem is hypothetical and artificial, it nevertheless draws Sarah in, eliciting some intriguing comments about the ethics of killing.

From the outset, Sarah personalizes the dilemma, shifting from the question of what the rifleman should do to the more concrete question of what *she* would probably do under these difficult circumstances. Her first response focuses on the fact that, as a member of the squad, she would have a special relationship with the other soldiers. Because they are comrades and friends, she would feel a special affection for them and a special obligation to them, so that in weighing a life against another life, she would decide in their favor. She feels at least slightly uncomfortable about this reasoning, however, characterizing it as selfishness. And, recognizing that killing an innocent woman would leave her distressed, she infers that there is something wrong about the act of killing someone to protect her comrades.

To further justify her choice, Sarah considers the "morals of war." It's not clear exactly what she believes these are, but the basic idea seems to be that war has its own set of rules, a special code for circumstances removed from everyday moral life, and that part of this code involves protecting friend against foe, doing what's best for your own side and not worrying about the other side.

In her response to my final question, Sarah first claims that no act is inherently right or wrong, but that the reasons for an action determine its morality. Since there is no absolute moral rule to tell a person what to do (for example, no absolute prohibition against killing), she suggests that all a person can do is try to determine what seems "best" in the circumstances. Earlier, she claims that a person has to have the moral courage to make choices that might turn out to be tragically "wrong" (to have bad consequences). But at the end of the transcript she seems to suggest two guidelines for deciding what to do in these circumstances, both of them oriented to the consequences of the act, though in different ways.

Sarah says first that she would feel greater grief and regret over the death of her friends than she would over the death of the woman: she couldn't "deal with" the idea that she choked and let her comrades get killed. In other words, Sarah is weighing the consequences of the two worst outcomes in terms of how much emotion and guilt she would feel. The fact that one outcome would produce so much more psychological pain than the other seems to justify shooting the woman. Finally, at the end of the transcript, Sarah mentions the discrepancy in the number of people who might be harmed in this situation: she would feel worse to let "a whole bunch of people die rather than one." The reasoning here seems to be a version of the "greatest good/least harm" principle—better for one to die than many.

In sum, Sarah brought a variety of ethical principles to bear on the Rifleman's Dilemma: she said that personal relationships count in ethical decisions, that the code of conduct for war may differ from the rules of everyday moral life, that personal guilt is an index of the morality of an act, and that an agent must weigh the outcomes and consequences of an action when making a moral decision. Sarah's classmates said many of the same things, although some focused more attention on the rifleman's duty as a lookout, and yet others tried to ascertain how likely it was that the woman posed a threat to the squad. Fascinated by the patterns of ethical reflection that I uncovered during these exploratory conversations, I decided to use the Rifleman's Dilemma again in the fall of 1986 and 1989, when I taught the course to large classes of freshmen—although I changed to a written-response format (rather than holding interviews). I hoped that their answers to the exercise would provide a reasonably accurate index of what college freshmen thought about the ethics of killing during war.

Like Sarah, most of the freshmen (more than 70 percent) decided that the rifleman should shoot the woman by the trail.[3] Although initially surprised by the consistency of these responses, I decided that the exercise was probably biased toward (or "pulled for") a decision to shoot the woman. It was simply harder to find reasons *not* to shoot. One could argue that it is *always* wrong to kill a person, regardless of circumstances; however, that kind of radical pacificism was foreign to most of my students. Another reason not to shoot is that soldiers are always obligated to spare the lives of innocent civilians. But was this woman innocent? At best, her actions seem ambiguous, her intentions undecidable. One could argue that she should be given the benefit of the doubt. But when they could not decide the woman's innocence, most students examined the two "worst case" outcomes: weighing the death of a possibly innocent woman against the destruction of a squad of comrades who are counting on the rifleman to protect them from danger. Given that choice, nearly all of them decided that it was better to be "safe than sorry": the rifleman had to shoot the suspicious woman.

However, I was less interested in students' decisions than in their reasoning about a problematic moral situation—the kind of situation that they would read about again, later in the course. Thus the dilemma gave me both a way to introduce students to ethical inquiry and also a way to elicit their moral reasoning and ethical orientations. (The freshmen also completed the exercise at the end of the semester; I will discuss those final responses later in the chapter.)

I designed the dilemma so that the rifleman has to choose either to spare the woman (and thereby risk the squad) or to kill the woman (and hope she's not an innocent bystander). Although a small number of students (always less than 10 percent) found a way around these two options, proposing an alternative solution, most of them accepted the stipulations of the problem, so that they felt compelled to decide whether the rifleman should shoot the woman or hold his fire.[4]

Students tended to provide three kinds of reasons to justify a decision to shoot or hold fire: figuring the odds, calculating the consequences, and doing one's duty. Quite often students used more than one of these strategies, and some used all three of them. But I want to examine each reasoning strategy separately, considering examples of each of the three main patterns of moral justification that I found in my freshmen's responses to the Rifleman's Dilemma at the beginning of the semester.

One way to make the decision is to determine how likely it is that the woman is a guerrilla soldier. A number of students seemed to reason in the following way: if it seems quite likely that the woman is a guerrilla, then Johnson should shoot, since in doing so he will simply be killing an enemy soldier (even if a woman) in order to protect his comrades; however, if it seems probable that the woman is an innocent villager, it is reasonable for Johnson to take the risk of holding his fire. About half of the freshmen in both courses tried to "figure the odds" as a way of deciding what Johnson should do.[5]

When I wrote the dilemma, I tried to make it difficult to determine the woman's status.[6] On the one hand, the dilemma states that the squad was "deep in enemy-controlled territory," where they could expect to encounter snipers, sappers, and guerrilla forces, so that the woman's movements—bending over the trail and then quickly moving into the underbrush—could be construed as hostile. On the other hand, "many innocent peasants" lived in the area, and if the woman had merely been picking something up from the trail, it would not be unreasonable for her to hide when she heard an American patrol approaching. Was this woman a guerrilla, intent on harming the squad? Or was she an innocent peasant, caught by happenstance in the vicinity of an American patrol? Most students concluded that she was very likely an enemy, citing several reasons for that conclusion.

The most frequent reason was simply that she was in "enemy-controlled" territory, where everyone should be distrusted.

If the enemy had control over an area it seems very unlikely that a woman would just happen to be strolling along. Most likely she was there for a purpose. [F/FR/F86]

Few students were convinced that the woman was innocently picking something up from the trail. The fact that she hid in the bushes meant that she was acting in a suspicious and incriminating manner.

The woman's quick, secretive movements indicated that she could very well be setting up a trap. If she was indeed avoiding American soldiers, then why did she not go deeply into the woods, instead of hiding by the edge of the road? [M/FR/F89]

Even when they recognized that the situation was ambiguous and that Johnson could not be certain, many still found the woman's actions sufficiently suspicious to conclude that she was probably a VC. And if there was a basis for concluding that she was an enemy, then Johnson was justified in shooting her.

While most of my freshmen tried to resolve the dilemma by figuring out the odds, nearly as many approached the problem through a different kind of calculation. These students attempted to weigh the consequences of Johnson's actions in the two "worst-case" outcomes: Johnson shoots the woman and she turns out to be innocent; Johnson holds his fire and the woman blows up the squad. For a number of students, the answer to the dilemma seemed to lie in assessing which of these two bad outcomes produces the least harm.[7] This strategy is particularly appropriate if one assumes that the circumstances are ambiguous, so that Johnson cannot be certain whether the woman is a peasant or a guerrilla. As one student put it: "Johnson really has no way of knowing whether or not she is innocent" [F/FR/F89]. And, she adds, in that situation "it is better to be safe than sorry"—a phrase that appeared frequently in the students' responses.

In a majority of cases, students who focused on the worst-case outcomes decided that Johnson should shoot the woman. But they arrived at this conclusion by two different routes. The most heavily travelled route involved some variation of the argument that one death is not as bad as many. Some expressed the argument in quantitative terms.

The death of one woman is inconsequential compared to the death of an infantry squad. [M/FR/F86]

Which is better in terms of cost, one life or many lives? [M/FR/F86]

Even if she was only a peasant, he cannot be sure, and by killing one woman he possibly saves the lives of twenty men. [F/FR/F86]

Others cited the familiar precept about the needs of many taking precedence over the needs of the few.

It is the right thing for him to do simply because "the needs of the many outweigh the needs of the few." [F/FR/F86]

The decision had to be made for the side of the many or for that of the one woman. Usually, the needs of the many should outweigh those of the few. [M/FR/F86]

The logic of this principle seemed unassailable to many students, so that it led to the only possible choice.

It is not necessarily the right thing to do; it is the only thing to do. By not shooting the woman, he is risking the life of a whole squad. If he shoots the woman, he is only taking a chance with her life. . . . The needs of the many outweigh the needs of one. [M/FR/F86]

A less frequent approach to the problem involved assessing the consequences for Johnson himself, especially weighing how much guilt he would feel in each of the two worst outcomes. For quite a few students, it seemed clear that Johnson would suffer the greatest personal harm if he stood by and watched his comrades get blown up. The strain on his conscience if he allowed the death of his friends seemed to outweigh any regret he would be likely to feel over killing an innocent peasant.

If Private Johnson was to hold back his fire and not shoot the woman, then he would have to answer to his conscience that he was responsible for the death of many of his men. . . . If he shot the woman, however, then his conscience would only have to deal with the death of one person, and that is an easier thing to deal with. [F/FR/F86]

In sum, when they focused on the consequences of Johnson's actions—whether they considered the consequences for others or the implications for his own peace of mind—the great majority of students concluded that Johnson ought to act so as to minimize the harm that his actions could cause. And that principle of minimizing harm (or its complement, protecting the greatest number of lives) seemed clearly to mean that the rifleman should shoot the woman.

In a third approach to the dilemma, a number of students considered Johnson's obligations and responsibilities.[8] First of all, Johnson has a general duty, as a soldier, to kill when required to do so. As one student put it, killing "comes with the territory and responsibility of being a soldier" [F/FR/F86]. Therefore, soldiers cannot continue to follow the same ethical principles that they learned to obey during peacetime.

During war I believe the soldiers had to do things to save their lives that if it weren't war time they would consider morally wrong—and to murder someone is wrong. War changes the rules, and to survive and protect each other . . . the issues of right and wrong must be put aside. [F/FR/F89]

Students seemed to reason as follows: according to our peacetime morality, killing another human being is the most immoral and heinous crime imaginable, but in war, killing other human beings is acceptable and possibly even virtuous. Therefore, war has different rules, and our old ideas about right and wrong are simply not applicable in that sphere.

In the situation that Private Johnson is facing, I see it fit for him to shoot. Under the circumstances of war, rules change. [F/FR/F89]

During war, particularly this war, people's values change to meet and survive in a hostile environment. . . . Old ideas of right and wrong don't necessarily apply here. [M/FR/F86]

Not only is Johnson committed to a special ethic because of his general responsibilities as a soldier but he also has a specific duty because of his assignment. Many students said that, when he was assigned as lookout, Johnson was entrusted with the lives of the soldiers in his squad, so that he has an obligation to protect them.

Johnson was a lookout. As a lookout he is in charge of "looking out" for any sign of trouble that he can see but his squad can't. The woman is a definite sign of trouble. He must take her life rather than have the chance of her taking the life of the squad. [M/FR/F89]

Private Johnson should shoot the woman because of the responsibility he has to his squad as being the lookout person. The squad leader gave him a duty, and he should fulfill the duty in the best interest of his men. Private Johnson has no room or time to put in his personal feelings for the woman. [F/FR/F86]

Johnson simply must find the moral courage to do his duty as a soldier and the assigned lookout, regardless of consequences— even if an innocent woman may die, even if he will regret it later, even if he has to live with her blood on his hands.

I feel it's the only thing he can do, because he has an obligation to the squad to secure their safety no matter what, even if an innocent woman dies. He might think it's wrong, but it's still his obligation. [M/FR/F86]

Although a majority of students found ways to justify shooting the woman, a small number (20 percent of the students in both 1986 and 1989) insisted that Johnson should not kill her. Some argued that there were too many uncertainties to justify taking a human life. The woman should be considered "innocent until proven guilty" and given the "benefit of the doubt" in the absence of strong proof concerning her intentions.

The idea of shooting someone when you're not sure if they are enemies is wrong and cruel. What would happen if the woman was just a peasant and had several small children and Johnson shot her? Is it justifiable to shoot someone just because they look suspicious? In my opinion it is not. [F/FR/F89]

From this perspective, if there is any chance that the woman may be innocent then the rifleman must obey a "higher law," according to which he has the obligation, both as a human being and a soldier, to protect the lives of those civilians who may be caught up in war through no fault of their own. Johnson may feel a stronger affiliation with his unit, his friends, people of his same race and nationality. But he must subordinate those feelings to his sense of what is right.

I love my comrades much more than some old evil lady that's gonna kill them. She is dirt. But, if I really feel in my mind that she is innocent or even if I sway towards her innocence, I won't kill her. [M/FR/F86]

For some students, it simply was not right to kill this woman: doing so would be "murder."

The lady did not demonstrate any resistance to the squad—only fear. He didn't actually see any mine or weapon, and therefore it would have been murder. You can't just shoot any person for being near your squad. Many Vietnamese people might live in the area; they might be truly innocent. [M/FR/F89]

To know what is right, Johnson should put himself in the woman's shoes or imagine how he would feel if the situation were reversed—if it were his wife or mother along the trail and an enemy lookout spotted her. Wouldn't he want her to be given the benefit of the doubt?

What if it had been America and a North Vietnamese soldier shot his wife for being in the road? [F/FR/F89]

But such worries were infrequent. Most of the students argued that Johnson has a chance to prevent disaster, and only a fool would split moral hairs when the lives of so many of his friends and comrades are at stake. The fact that Johnson's *friends* are in jeopardy was an important consideration for some students.[9] As one freshman put it, the resolution to the dilemma might be quite different if one had to consider only Johnson and the woman on the trail:

If the situation only involved Private Johnson and the woman, things would have been different. However, there were many more people involved—his friends. If I was in this situation (and there was just the lady and me), I would have not shot her. Yet, since I had to defend my friends against enemies, I would kill the lady. I can handle losing my life in a war, but I could not handle being responsible for other Americans' lives, especially my friends. [F/FR/F89]

For these students, Johnson should shoot the woman not just because many lives are at risk, but because the lives in question are people with whom he has bonds of affiliation and affection.

For most of the freshmen in my courses, the dilemma facing the rifleman was susceptible to rational resolution. Many of the students examined the circumstances carefully and weighed the outcomes judiciously. Although some students merely toted up the dead like tokens in a game, most tried to assess the larger ramifications of the deaths or attempted to reckon with broader consequences. While some students may have had a rigid conception of duty, that the lookout could do anything to protect his squad, others conceived of Johnson's responsibilities in more complex ways, recognizing his obligation both to protect truly innocent civilians and to look out for the safety of his comrades. And most of these students offered multiple reasons for their decisions—reasons that, if not always sophisticated, were often surprisingly mature for freshmen in their first weeks of college.

Nevertheless, the students' responses provide only a partial, and perhaps even a skewed, picture of their capacity for ethical reflection. The Rifleman's Dilemma may have been the kind of problem that poses the fewest difficulties for students. As Rosenblatt argues, it is easiest for students to "think rationally" about an impersonal exercise, a problem devoid of emotional coloring or personal connection. Indeed, a number of the freshmen seemed to attack the dilemma like a puzzle: systematically, but without urgency. Where, then, do students find a context for the kind of fervent rationality that ethical inquiry seems to demand? In Rosenblatt's view, "That kind of rationality may be fostered by literature" (*Literature as Exploration* 227). For many students, Philip Caputo's memoir, *A Rumor of War*, provided that context.

Caputo tries to explain how a "good" American college boy could end up being tried for the murder of two Vietnamese civilians. Caputo's transformation began in Marine boot camp, where he and his comrades chanted such slogans as "Ambushes are murder and murder is fun." Once in Vietnam, however, his early enthusiasm about being a soldier was gradually destroyed by a struggle in which the principal enemy was not the VC but the inhospitable terrain, the insufferable heat, and the merciless mines that cut the Marines to pieces without giving them any opportunity to retaliate.

At the height of Caputo's exhaustion and frustration, one of his men, a soldier named Crowe, reports that he has discovered two Viet Cong in a nearby village. Crowe claims that a Vietnamese boy, Le Dung, has identified two of the villagers as sappers who are engaged in making mines and booby traps. Although these two Vietnamese had been previously interrogated and cleared as draft-dodgers, Caputo cannot shake his conviction that they must be responsible for the deaths of his men. He decides to take action.

One night Caputo is supposed to send a patrol to an ambush site near the suspects' village, but he tells his men that if no one walks into the ambush, they should go into the village and get the two Vietnamese suspects, killing them if they resist. As he looked into the face of Allen, the patrol leader, Caputo "knew he was going to kill those men on the slightest pretext" (300).

The next passage in the book is crucial. Caputo claims that it "was my secret and savage desire that the two men die" (300). Later, Allen reports by radio that the patrol has killed one VC and captured the other. As they approach the perimeter, the patrol shoots the prisoner, claiming that he made an attempt to escape. But when they bring the body in, Caputo sees that it is the Vietnamese informant, the boy named Le Dung.

The soldiers act nervous and guilty. Caputo asks Crowe if he is certain that the body on the ground is one of the VC. Crowe says that he is sure, but he will not look Caputo in the eye. Caputo recoils in guilt and horror at what has happened. He says, "They had killed the wrong man. No, not they; *we. We* had killed the wrong man. That boy's innocent blood was on my hands as much as it was on theirs" (304).

Caputo and his men are charged with murder. Although in the passage above he seems to admit his complicity in the killing, in the last part of the book Caputo considers all the reasons that neither he nor his men are truly to blame for the deaths of the two Vietnamese. He argues that the war itself is principally to blame. Although he recognizes that "there was murder in my heart," he cannot "conceive of the act as one of premeditated murder," because "the thing we had done was a result of what the war had done to us" (309). In Caputo's mind, the conditions under which the war was being fought explain his actions. There were the mines that had taken the lives of so many men, with no chance for retaliation. There was the physical and mental exhaustion of jungle warfare. There was the constant pressure to produce bodies, the rewards for displaying initiative and aggressiveness. In that environment, "everything rotted and corroded quickly . . . bodies, boot leather, canvas, metal, morals" (217).

In pressing charges against him, the military is less concerned with truth or justice, Caputo believes, than it is with protecting its image and safeguarding its illusions. As Caputo sums up the military-justice proceedings: "The war in general and U.S. military policies in particular were ultimately to blame for the deaths. . . . That was the truth and it was that truth which the whole proceeding was designed to conceal" (313). In the end, the charges against Caputo are dropped. He is given a letter of reprimand and sent home.

A Rumor of War gave students an opportunity to reflect once again on such issues as how to define "murder" in war and how to determine a soldier's guilt or innocence.

> When [Caputo] was put on trial for killing Le Dung, I had a hard time deciding if what he had done was excusable or not. In my mind I kept thinking that what had happened was an honest mistake. He sent the men into the village to find the two VC. It's the fact that he had murder on his mind, which is wrong. But was it wrong because they shot an innocent person or because it was premeditated? . . . In war, I think that it would be very hard to decide if a killing was murder or not. . . . Murder in war is not clearly defined and occurs under different circumstances. In an atmosphere of killing, it is very hard to determine which killing is right and which killing is wrong. [F/FR/F86]

When students engaged in this kind of ethical inquiry in their journals, I tried to write encouraging and supportive comments: "good thinking here" or "you're wrestling with some difficult issues—keep up the good work." But I also tried to challenge their thinking by raising issues and questions. For example, a student wrote the following reflection on war as murder.

> Murder. Murder is a pretty serious word. Except when it comes to war. War is murder. In every war since the beginning of time, people have been murdered. [F/FR/F86]

In the margin I commented:

> What's the difference between killing and murder? Is all killing of humans murder? When a policeman shoots a terrorist? Can there be both killing and murder in war? Is one worse than the other?

By raising these kinds of questions, I tried to prevent students from reaching premature closure on the issues we were considering.

For many students, the central question was how to judge Caputo. Most of them tended to be swayed more by Caputo's enumeration of "extenuating circumstances" than by his confession that Le Dung's "innocent blood" was on his hands.

Caputo . . . thought he was sending his men out to get the VC which were the enemy. He had good reason to believe this and his duty was to try and get them. Secondly, when he does find out it is the young boy, he has a change of attitude right then, which sets him apart from the rest of his men, who were still laughing and joking. He may have been wrong in trying to cover it up, but to defend his troops is also a very understandable stance. [M/SR/S86]

And students were persuaded by Caputo's suggestion that the ultimate responsibility for the killings rested with the military and the people who decided to wage the war in the first place.

Philip Caputo found out about "murder" when he ordered the execution of two possible Viet Cong soldiers. . . . Caputo probably should have been arrested (as he was), but who is to blame? The "higher ups" who ordered bodies, bodies, bodies? . . . I think that the government and the "higher ups" are to blame. [F/FR/F86]

Caputo was trained by his country to kill. Now his country wants to put him in prison for it. Does the military teach a moral way of killing? I do not believe so. They teach boys murdering is "fun." They seem to be hypocrites. They told Caputo to murder and he did; now they are trying to punish him for it. [F/FR/F89]

Because they sympathized with Caputo, many students were shocked that the military would charge him with murder. One freshman put it bluntly: "Those charges brought up against Caputo and his men were a real crock of shit" [M/FR/F86]. And a number of other students seemed incredulous that anyone could condemn Caputo or his men for their actions.

How can a soldier be accused of murdering a Vietnamese during war? It seems impossible! I sat there reading, totally agreeing with Caputo, and I was as astonished and as confused about the situation as he was. It's war and from what I have learned by reading, about the only thing for a soldier to do was kill, and that was his job. They're taught to kill, so how can someone commit a murder? [F/FR/F86]

The ending was a real shock. I totally did not expect Caputo to be tried for murder! The deaths . . . just seemed like other tragedies of the war. To me, it seems like that kind of stuff happened all the time—either accidentally or not. The idea of trying someone for murder in the middle of a war is totally insane! [F/FR/F89]

One of the pedagogical issues I had to face at about this point in the course was whether I should reveal my own ethical judgments—and if so, how. On the one hand, I didn't want to impose moral values on students, and I certainly didn't want to preempt ethical inquiry by revealing my views. On the other hand, I didn't want to create the impression that one could maintain a position of neutrality on the serious moral issues we were considering. In the end, I decided to express my views as undogmatically as possible.

I revealed my own struggle to make judgments about acts of killing in war, explaining that while I empathized a great deal with the ambiguities and frustrations our soldiers faced in Vietnam, I also believed that distinctions could be—*must* be—made between killing and murder. As former Marine lieutenant William Broyles says so clearly and emphatically: "Even though the line between killing and murder is not always easy to define, any soldier knows the difference. Murder is different from killing" (*Brothers* 240).

Caputo's case is, nonetheless, vexing for me. To begin with, I can all too easily imagine myself in his shoes. As a young lieutenant, I had many of Caputo's attitudes and characteristics. And in his circumstances, I might well have done the same things he did. But that would not make them right. The two Vietnamese were not killed; they were murdered. Although it seems too harsh to assign all the blame to Caputo, it seems too lenient to dismiss the incident as an inevitable result of the war. Because the "line" is not so easy to define in Caputo's circumstances, I hoped that *A Rumor of War* would elicit a complex, but also compassionate, process of ethical inquiry. In any case, that is the orientation I tried to exemplify in my own moral deliberations, an orientation that Rosenblatt captures in her discussion of the kind of ethical inquiry that literary texts can foster:

> Instead of simply approving or condemning, one might seek to understand. Instead of fixed rules of conduct unconditionally applied to all under all circumstances, judgment should be passed only after the motives of the behavior and the particular circumstances had been understood. One might condemn the act and yet wish to understand what produced it. Moral judgment itself would thus become more humane. (*Literature as Exploration* 233)

Although Caputo's book sparked considerable discussion of the ethics of killing, it nevertheless persuaded some students that war is a sphere of human action that is inherently irrational and immoral. Because I wanted them to think more carefully about this view, I designed some activities to elicit further inquiry into the morality of killing during war.

In my freshman courses I started one class by asking students to respond, in writing, to a statement on a worksheet that I handed out at the beginning of the hour:

Some people claim that it is futile and senseless to try to make ethical judgments about events or actions in war. By definition, war is without morality—an activity in which anything goes— so that our usual judgments of right or wrong, good or evil, simply do not apply to it. Caputo seems, at times, to espouse this view. For example, in the Prologue to *A Rumor of War* he says that it was "the dawn of creation in the Indochina bush, an ethical as well as a geographical wilderness" (xx). And he admits to feeling "contempt" for people who want to make ethical distinctions or impose a "code of battlefield ethics that attempted to humanize an essentially inhuman war" (218). Do you agree? Can actions in war be subject to moral assessment?

Ethical Inquiry

I gave students about ten minutes to write a response to this question on the bottom of the worksheet. When they finished, I told them to put their comments away, adding this piece of writing to their journals. (Quite a few of these sheets never made it into the journals, however.)

With their attention focused by the exercise, I tried to provoke students' thinking about whether moral judgments serve any purpose in a combat zone. And to challenge the idea that soldiers' actions are always beyond moral assessment, I asked students to consider some cases of truly heinous acts. I usually read aloud an excerpt from *Nam*, Mark Baker's collection of oral histories, in which a soldier describes his participation in a brutal act of rape, murder, and dismemberment.[10] According to the story, a patrol of grunts was coming in from twenty hard days in the field when they encountered a Vietnamese man and a teenage girl riding on a motorbike. The soldiers stopped the pair and searched them, finding only a can of Army-issue pears, which the man claimed he had received at the base where he worked. The soldiers first opened the pears and ate them. Then they gang-raped the girl. Next they shot the man, "pumping rounds into him until the guy just busts open. He didn't have a face anymore." Then they shot the sobbing girl, stomped the bodies with their boots, and finally carved off various body parts—ears, noses, fingers, breasts—as souvenirs. The teller of the tale comments: "And everybody was laughing about it."

The lecture hall was silent when I stopped reading. I waited for the shock to sink in, for the implications to reverberate. Faced with this example of unmotivated brutality, it is difficult to maintain that war justifies any and all acts.

Later, when I collected their journals, I looked for the sheets that I had handed out in the lecture, asking whether actions in war can be subject to moral assessment. Although I did not examine journals from every student in the course, and not every journal contained the sheet, I found that a sizeable majority said that war is a realm beyond moral judgment. Students presented three arguments for that position. The first was that war cannot be understood by those who have not seen it firsthand. As civilians (and eighteen-year-old college freshmen), some students felt inadequate to render moral judgments about soldiers' actions.

I agree that we can't, as civilians who have not been to war, make ethical judgments about events or actions in war. There are so many obstacles and factors that we aren't aware of. . . . We can't apply ordinary standards we might have set for certain situations to one that might occur during war. . . . Vietnam was such a devastating experience that I don't think I have the knowledge or right to judge them. [F/FR/F86]

Another argument was that anything goes in war because the only object is to survive and win—it doesn't matter what you have to do to achieve your objectives.

No, actions of war cannot be subject to moral assessment. Those men were paid to kill and if it meant killing innocent people that is what they did. Their officers didn't care who they killed, just as long as there was a high body count. The old saying is very true: that all is fair in love and war. Nobody can be held responsible for their actions when they are cut loose and told to be like animals. [M/FR/F86]

Yet another line of reasoning was that it makes no sense to try to differentiate between moral and immoral acts of killing. War inevitably involves killing—an inherently immoral act—and so the whole enterprise is already so evil that individual actions cannot possibly be judged as right or wrong.

No, I don't agree that actions in war can be subject to moral assessment. War is built on evil. It thrives on evil. The men are trained to kill and rewarded to kill. It is hard to see a difference between killing one person and killing another. Either way the same act is being committed, an act that is supposed to be done in a war. When Caputo was put on trial for accidentally killing the wrong people, I thought it was almost funny. [F/FR/F86]

In a number of cases, however, I found that the incident of unmotivated brutality that I read later in the period had challenged students to reconsider their views. In some cases, students wrote about that change in their journals:

I just reread what I wrote in class today. I sound like a horrible, bloodthirsty beast! After what Dr. Kroll read to us in class from *Nam*, I felt sick. And after rereading what I had written earlier, it could be inferred that I approved of what was read. This isn't so! Too bad I didn't write in pencil, right? But that's really what I thought at the beginning of class! How could I change? Especially so quickly? [M/FR/F89]

Other students added comments on the bottom of the response sheets—directly beneath their initial reactions. For example, at the beginning of the class one freshman wrote that he did not believe that acts of war could be subject to moral assessment, because a soldier's "mission is to kill" and because what might seem wrong to a civilian could be "what a soldier thinks he needs to do to survive." Later, at the bottom of his response sheet, the student wrote:

My ignorance got me again. Your points were well made. My original idea of a moral-less act was shooting somebody twice instead of just once (or something like that). Then the quotes you read surprised the heck out of me. [M/FR/F86]

In other cases, the students' additional comments evince a more radical reorientation. For example, at the beginning of the lecture one woman wrote the following statement concerning the issue of whether actions in war can be subject to moral assessment.

I agree with Caputo. Anything goes in war as long as it doesn't embarrass the U.S. government. There is no right or wrong in war because everything is already wrong. Everything is already screwed up. Vietnam messed up the lives of EVERYONE involved. Another dead civilian didn't matter. There was no murder—killing was just part of the game the U.S. decided to play.

Our government didn't have the right to judge the actions of any soldier. [F/FR/F86]

Not long after the lecture, apparently, the student added the following comments to the same sheet.

After Kroll's lecture and various readings I have changed my mind. In war people are still human beings. . . . The things soldiers did to civilians were incredibly horrible. Sure, these soldiers . . . had it bad, especially the U.S. [soldiers] who didn't even want to be there. But the civilians had it just as bad and it was worse for them. Young girls didn't have military training or a way to protect themselves against rape. . . . And I was wrong; another dead civilian *does* matter.

My aim was to challenge those students who had too readily accepted the argument that war is beyond good and evil, that it is a sphere of activity removed from moral deliberation and ethical inquiry.

The My Lai Massacre provided another useful case for discussion. One semester I asked my students to read some articles about My Lai, and another time I showed a documentary about the massacre. In both cases, however, the incident provoked serious thinking about the necessity for moral judgments in war. Many students condemned the slaughter in no uncertain terms.

I would imagine that many people don't think war can have murders, but I do. Those people were murdered . . . and I think it is unforgivable. [F/SR/S88]

They killed children who could barely walk—much less support the VC. To me, they had to have been able to realize that what they were doing was very wrong. [F/SO/S88]

But others were reluctant to condemn the soldiers who had participated in the massacre. Some felt they had no right to judge a situation that they had not confronted themselves.

Ethical Inquiry

If I wasn't actually at My Lai, how could I judge others' actions? I didn't go through the physical and emotional upheavals that the soldiers endured daily. [F/FR/F89]

And some argued that the men at My Lai were not really responsible for their actions.

Lieutenant Calley's actions in My Lai were unacceptable by any standards. But I ask myself, OK, here is a man who has or had the ability to kill defenseless men, women, and children. Would this same man be able to do this without a war going on around him? Military training? If not, is this man truly responsible for his actions? [M/SR/S88]

Judging from the journals, most students were disturbed and perplexed by what happened at My Lai: they were truly horrified by the senseless slaughter of women and children.[11] And yet, they also empathized with the plight of American soldiers, trapped in a terrifying guerrilla war. Some students worried about how they might behave in similar circumstances.

Would I have done the same thing in their place or would I have refused to do it? I'd really like to think that I wouldn't, but I also really hope I'm never put in a situation where I would have to find out. [F/FR/F89]

In short, the massacre asked students to think about moral issues in the context of conflicting emotions. The struggle to reconcile discrepant sentiments is particularly clear in the following journal entry.

I don't quite understand how I feel about the incident or maybe I can't decide. Sometimes I feel sorry for the men who were there, as if they had no control over their actions. But then I think that everyone should be responsible for their actions. . . . They can't say that it was the war that made them do it, because that would be a major cop-out. It would excuse everything. But the problem is that the effects of that type of warfare on the men *did* have something to do with it. How else can you explain why a platoon of soldiers transformed into a mob of crazed killers in an instant? This whole problem is so frustrating because I can't come up with answers to all my questions! [F/FR/F89]

This kind of wrestling with ethical complexity is precisely what I hoped to encourage in the course. And I was pleased when students' thinking about My Lai fed back into their reflections on their reading.

Before the movie about the My Lai Massacre, I didn't think Caputo should have been charged with murder. My Lai was the Caputo incident multiplied. . . . Why is it all right for two people to be killed and not all right for four hundred? . . . It is just as wrong for one wrong murder as it is for four hundred wrong murders. At the end of *A Rumor of War* I did not feel that Caputo should have been charged, but after the movie I had serious doubts. [F/FR/F89]

Later in the semester, students read other books in which there are disturbing incidents of killing. In *Born on the Fourth of July*, Ron Kovic tells how, during a night ambush, his patrol shot into a hut of suspected sappers, only to discover that it was full of women and children. In *Going After Cacciato*, Tim O'Brien tells how a squad "fragged" their gung-ho lieutenant because he insisted that they search tunnels before destroying them. But perhaps the most provocative incident is in James Webb's novel, *Fields of Fire*, a book that I assigned in both of my smaller classes.

In one of the central episodes in Webb's book, a squad leader called Snake takes his men in search of the VC who have ambushed and carried off two of their comrades (Baby Cakes and Ogre). They find an old man and a young woman in a nearby village, where they also discover the buried remains of their two friends. Although the Vietnamese claim they are innocent—that the VC made them bury the bodies—they appear to be guilty, and so the squad executes them. Only one of the Americans protests, a Harvard-educated misfit named Goodrich. After the incident, Goodrich is wracked by guilt: "There's no way to justify murder. The rules say kill, O.K. But when the rules say stop, you've got to stop. We're not God. We're not barbarians" (335). Goodrich later reports the incident to the authorities. But before charges can be pressed, the squad members who were involved are killed or badly wounded in a battle.

Students tended to compare the killings in *Fields of Fire* to the ones in *A Rumor of War*. In both cases, there are questions about whether the soldiers have done anything seriously wrong in seeking retribution.

The part about Baby Cakes and Ogre brings up a moral question similar to that which we saw in Caputo. This dilemma doesn't seem near as bad as Caputo's to me, however. Maybe it is the way the book was written, but it doesn't seem as big of an atrocity. To me, the evidence is pretty clear cut, it is circumstantial but overwhelmingly so. Another point is that the murder was not premeditated. . . . The big difference between Caputo's episode and Webb's is that in Caputo's I would like to think I would refrain [from the killings], whereas in Webb's, I could picture myself participating in the killings if two of my best friends had been killed. [M/SR/S86]

But the incident in Webb's book raises an additional question: whether Goodrich has done the right thing to report the episode to the authorities.

This question is embedded in a web of contrasting ethical orientations that come to light when Goodrich's approach to morality is compared with the moral order that prevails among the men in his unit. In brief, Goodrich is the spokesman for principled morality, for the view that ethical judgments can and must be made in war. For Goodrich, being "good" means acting in accordance with principles. But because of his principles, Goodrich is portrayed as a disconnected individual, a man cut off from sustaining relationships and from commitments to other persons. Although his disconnection from the unit appears to give Goodrich the autonomy he needs in order to contradict and condemn the actions of others in his platoon, his principled ethic leaves him isolated, self-centered, and unable to risk himself to help others in distress.

By contrast, the moral order of the platoon is grounded in a group ethic, according to which the good of the unit gives meaning to an individual's actions and takes precedence over them. Being "good" means being willing to sacrifice your own safety for the welfare of others in your unit—to expose yourself to hostile fire to save the wounded, for example, as Snake does repeatedly in the novel, even sacrificing his life to rescue Goodrich during the final battle. However, the unit's ethic subordinates principled morality (a concept of what is "right") to the group's welfare (its own "good"), so that there seems to be no moral referent beyond the group and its self-preservation. From the platoon's viewpoint, Goodrich should protect his comrades, even if he has misgivings about their deeds.

Students debated the merits of the two approaches to morality that they encountered in *Fields of Fire*. Some condemned Goodrich and felt that his principled ethic was out of place in Vietnam.

Goodrich thinks too much of what is right or wrong. He pays too much attention to conventional principles and that seems to be dangerous in a war situation. There are times for principles and when they should govern your behavior. Like in a normal social situation. . . . But there are times when you have to act from your instincts. And not worry so much about the conventions of right vs. wrong behavior. [F/JR/S88]

But others saw value in both an ethic of principles and an ethic of group solidarity, and they struggled to find ways to integrate these two approaches.

I think that the idea of a group/community morality sounds good . . . but I think . . . there has to be a mix. The guys in the group . . . have to keep some of their individual principles in order to know where to draw the line when choices have to be made. The group can't just capture a VC and say, "I think it was this guy who put a bullet in Johnny's head," and since it might as well have been my head, we should shoot up his head. I'm sure that must be really rough and that they would want revenge, but there also has to be some sort of justice involved. I repeat, there have got to be limits in war, and I don't think a group pumping each other up to kill can see those limits unless they look at a situation from an individual standpoint as well as the group's. [F/SR/S88]

Thus in several reading and writing assignments throughout the course, students confronted moral dilemmas and engaged in ethical reflection. Then, at the end of the semester, I asked the freshmen to respond to the Rifleman's Dilemma a second time. I wanted them to reconsider the rifleman's decision now that they had the course behind them. And I also wanted to compare what they said at the end of the semester with what they had written at the beginning of the course.

When I compared responses from the beginning and end of the course, I found that only a small number of students (20 percent) changed their decisions about the dilemma. Those who changed their minds often claimed that a key factor was learning that women sometimes played a role in the guerrilla fighting in Vietnam. When the odds increased that the woman on the trail was a VC, it tipped the scales in favor of shooting her to protect the rifleman's comrades. In the following example, a student explains why she changed her decision from "don't shoot" at the beginning of the course to "shoot" at the end.[12]

I changed my decision about what Private Johnson should do because I was very naive about the VC at the beginning of the course. Because she was a woman, I thought she would be innocent, probably a villager. After reading many accounts about women who were VC, I realized that a woman in Vietnam was just as likely to be a VC as a man would be. . . . In my first response . . . I didn't really have much knowledge about how the VC operated, and didn't realize they could act as innocent villagers. [F/FR/F89]

In small number of cases, students changed their decisions from "shoot" to "don't shoot."[13] Usually, one of their explanations was that they had gained sympathy for the Vietnamese as human beings:

I'm still very unsure about what Johnson should do, but I changed my decision anyway. I did so because now I feel more opposed [to] killing than before. I felt from what I read that she was most likely innocent. We've seen and read about so many innocent people getting killed that I decided I wouldn't want her killed. . . . that's a person, and I wouldn't want any innocent person shot. What I've read in this course has changed my views. The Vietnamese were people—not just the enemy. [F/FR/F89]

Overall, however, students tended to make the same decisions and to use about the same kinds of justifications at the beginning and end of the course. A majority said that the rifleman should shoot the woman, and in fact more students made this decision at the end of the course.[14] In justifying their decisions, approximately the same percentage of students considered the consequences of the rifleman's actions (shooting or holding his fire).[15] However, a smaller percentage referred to conceptions of duty or responsibility at the end of the semester,[16] while a larger percentage weighed the odds that the woman was intending to harm the soldiers on the patrol.[17]

Although most students retained their original decisions and justifications, one should not conclude that the course had no influence on their deliberations. In fact, a number of students said that their responses at the end of the course, even when they were nearly identical to earlier responses, had been affected by the things they had read and learned about the war. Some students claimed that they were "more certain" that their responses were right or "felt more strongly" that their decisions were correct; others believed that their reasons, although essentially the same, were "better informed" at the end of the semester; and yet others felt that their views, though unaltered, had undergone intense scrutiny during the course. For example, below are responses from two students whose decisions were the same at both points in the semester.

Ethical Inquiry

My decision [both times] was for Johnson to hold his fire, and I feel more strongly about it now than I did at the start of the course. It seems there was so much needless killing during the war (e.g., Kovic's shooting the corporal and the massacre of the children). During the course many things I have heard, watched, and read have affected my decision. The Kovic book was one of them. Another was an excerpt Dr. Kroll read to us out of a book. It was about a girl and her father, I believe, telling how the girl was raped and beaten and then both killed by American soldiers, for no reason. The more I hear about these incidents, the stronger my opinion becomes. Even during war you can't justify taking human life on a guess. [F/FR/F86]

I feel [again] that the choice had to be to kill the woman, because it was, unfortunately, a time of war and Johnson was left with few other alternatives that would assure the safety of his men. The course did make this decision all the more difficult, because of the large amount of time devoted to discussing the ethics of war and killing. A very high value should be placed on every human life; and that life and a person's innocence should be preserved. This course, however, taught us that each situation must be judged individually since each circumstance has its own consequences and ethical implications. And because of the situation, it's in the best interest of the squad to shoot her. [F/FR/F89]

In sum, the Rifleman's Dilemma was an important exercise because it stimulated ethical reasoning and gave students an opportunity to reflect on their responses to a moral dilemma. In addition, their responses provided me with a useful overview of students' orientations to the kind of situation the rifleman faced. But the dilemma was, in many cases, a poor gauge of both the intensity with which students engaged in ethical inquiry and the impact of the course on their moral deliberations. Let me illustrate by considering the way the course encouraged ethical reflection in Karen, the freshman from whom I've quoted in previous chapters. If Karen expressed her ideas more clearly than some of her peers, she nonetheless addressed many of the same issues, with about the same orientation, as many of the students in my classes.

In her initial response to the Rifleman's Dilemma, Karen said that Johnson should shoot the Vietnamese woman who was hiding by the trail. To justify her decision, Karen focused on Johnson's responsibility: given his "duty and obligation to the squad leader and the infantry squad, Johnson has no choice." Although there is a "good possibility" that the woman is an innocent peasant, there is an equally good possibility that she is planting a mine, since the Viet Cong used women in such roles. Therefore, Johnson must do his duty as a soldier and "try to save the lives of his fellow Americans."

At the end of the semester, Karen's answers were essentially the same: on both occasions she said that the rifleman should shoot the woman, and both times she justified that decision primarily on the basis of Private Johnson's duty to protect the members of his squad. In fact, when Karen compared her two responses to the dilemma, she said that she "didn't change [her] decision" and "gave essentially the same reasons." But on closer examination, it is clear that the experience of ethical inquiry had an impact on Karen's reflections on the Rifleman's Dilemma.

When she compared her two responses to the dilemma, Karen began by noting that she had, during the semester, changed her position on moral assessment.

Before this course I would have said there was no "right" or "wrong" in war, no possibility of judging morality. However, now I feel differently. There is a wrong kind of killing in war; there is murder—murder which should be punished. . . . The one story of the squad of men which stopped a man and his daughter who were riding their bikes, raped the daughter, ripped up their ID cards and killed them, is certainly an example of murder that should be punished, for those two Vietnamese posed absolutely no threat to the men.

But Karen can also conceive of other circumstances, ones that involve "killing that is directly related to the war." And, in Karen's view, that is the kind of situation in which Johnson finds himself in the Rifleman's Dilemma. Whereas the father and daughter posed no threat to soldiers, the woman hiding by the trail did.

This woman in Johnson's dilemma, however, did indeed pose a threat. There was the very real possibility that she was an enemy, that she did plant a booby trap or mine or in some way could endanger the lives of the men in Johnson's squad. In Vietnam, as many accounts attested, it was extremely difficult to know who exactly was the enemy. Many "innocent Vietnamese citizens" were actually VC spies or guerrilla soldiers.

Thus at the end of the course, Karen arrived at the same decision she had reached at the beginning:

Johnson's responsibility was to his squad, to see to it that they were unharmed. In this situation, the only decision which fulfilled this responsibility was to shoot the woman. This decision would be justified.

But her reasoning is clearly better informed and more complex at the end of the course. Let me trace the evolution of that reasoning as it is revealed in Karen's journal entries.

At the beginning of the course, Karen endorsed an ethical view that was widespread among students: the view that war is an arena beyond morality. Karen stated her initial position in the following entry:

I went in [to the course] truly believing that it was impossible to determine what was morally "right" or "wrong" in war. . . . Although I do not think I had a completely "anything goes" attitude, my belief was very close. I truly thought that since the purpose in war and certainly in the Vietnam War was to kill and in typical society killing is morally wrong, then how could anything done in war be judged on its morality. The whole concept of war is immoral.

When she read about the incident in *A Rumor of War*, Karen was surprised that anyone would blame Caputo for what he and his men had done. She found the whole idea of bringing him to trial "ludicrous."

I must say I was extremely shocked when I read that Caputo was charged with murder and was actually to be tried in court. Just as he said, he was told to kill, he did kill, and then he was quite possibly going to be punished for killing. It seemed ludicrous.

We see this same view in Karen's response to the worksheet that I distributed at the beginning of a lecture, asking students to comment on whether actions in war could be subject to moral assessment. Here is what she wrote:

When the sole purpose of war, particularly of the Vietnam War, was to kill the enemy—an essentially immoral act—how can one find anything moral about war let alone judge if something is moral or not? Considering the "right" thing to do in war is kill to win—which itself is morally "wrong"—there cannot be such a distinction between "right" and "wrong" on the battlefield. The same moral questions that are asked and judged upon in everyday society do not and cannot be asked in a war situation; they simply do not apply. Therefore, to try to determine the morality of an action in war is impossible and by far unreasonable.

Karen states the logic of her position quite well. However, it was precisely that view of war as a sphere beyond moral judgment that I wanted to challenge, hoping that students would reconsider their positions, opening their minds to a more complex world of moral reflection.

I challenged students' moral thinking by reading them the graphic account of the brutal killing of two Vietnamese by a group of American soldiers. At the beginning of the class, Karen had written on the worksheet that it was impossible to determine the morality of an action in war. But after the class, she made a series of journal entries that reveal a change of view. On the same day that she attended the lecture, Karen made the following entry:

146

Ethical Inquiry

At the beginning of today's lecture, I couldn't see the reasonableness in charging someone with murder in a war. It didn't make any sense to me. However, I only thought of soldiers killing because they had to—in self-defense, or by orders to kill the enemy, of course. A situation like the horrible one Mr. Kroll read in class did not occur to me. This account of the killing . . . and hacking them up made me sick to my stomach. Hearing this I know and now believe that there certainly should be "rules" of morality in war. There, indeed, do exist circumstances in which a soldier in war should be charged with and punished for murder. There do exist immoral acts of murder in a war. My naive and innocent eyes just couldn't see or want to see them.

Two days later, Karen's views were challenged again when she watched a videotape on the My Lai Massacre. She comments:

Just when I think I know enough about Vietnam (in terms of being exposed to different experiences and different viewpoints) so as not to be surprised about new information, something somewhat unbelievable is brought to our attention and I feel naive, almost ignorant. . . . My Lai opened my eyes wider. (I feel as if I am always saying this.)

Learning about My Lai reinforced her views that there could be "wrong" in war. Karen says of the massacre: "In my mind it is completely indefensible." Nevertheless, she felt conflicted, torn between her conviction that the massacre was wrong and her reluctance to assign guilt to one factor or person. She wrote in her journal:

I have an extremely difficult time pointing the finger and putting blame on specific people for the massacre at My Lai. Indeed, many factors have to be considered, and many fingers could be pointed. The U.S. government, captains, commanding officers on and off the field, soldiers, brainwashing or army training, the war, death, the weather, enemy, fatigue, razzled nerves—maybe it's simply best to recognize the fact that it was a mistake and not try to use any one person or group of people as a scapegoat. Then again, there are those who might not feel it was wrong. It is difficult for me to in the slightest bit comprehend how anyone could feel this massacre is justified in any way.

At the end of the semester, students were asked to write a "retrospective essay," a short paper that focused on some of the important issues they had considered during the course. Karen's essay was titled "Killing or Murder?" In it, she discussed in some detail the transformation of her views about the validity of moral judgment in war. The key is a distinction she learned to make between justifiable "killing" and the "murder" of people who pose no immediate threat. Karen claimed her views changed when she heard the story of the rape, murder, and dismemberment of the two Vietnamese civilians.

To me, this was wrong, very wrong, even in a war. The two Vietnamese posed no threat to the platoon, and what they did was murder, murder for which they should have been punished. Just as I had agreed with Caputo in the beginning of the course, I agreed with what William Broyles, Jr., wrote in his book, *Brothers in Arms*: "[But even though] in war the line between killing and murder is not always easy to define, any soldier knows the difference. Murder is different from killing" (240).

And in the final paragraph of her paper, Karen summed up her experience with ethical inquiry.

Although I consider myself rather fickle for this complete turn-around in belief, at the beginning of the course I was certainly ignorant in regards to the Vietnam War and all that happened. I came into the course steadfast in the belief that war is wrong, immoral, and that everything in war is wrong; therefore, it was ridiculous to punish a soldier for doing something wrong, like killing. This "anything goes" attitude, however, prevented me from seeing the fine but definite line between murder and killing that does exist in war. This course served as my magnifying glass and focused my eyes on the fact that a soldier's duty in war, particularly in the Vietnam War, was to kill, but not, however, to murder, unjustly and immorally.

Ethical Inquiry

Karen provides a clear example of the ways in which the course elicited reflection on the moral status of killing in war. What I tried to encourage was a view of ethical inquiry that differed from both the rigid moral absolutism that many students learned as children (and some brought with them to college) and the naive ethical relativism that they found among their peers at a state university, where moral values were treated as matters of individual taste. By asking students to confront some hard cases, especially in the novels, I hoped they would discover something about the complexity of moral situations. And by asking them to make reasoned judgments about those cases, I hoped students would learn that, despite complexity, there could be a reflective basis for deciding what is right and wrong. Sarah, the junior whose response to the Rifleman's Dilemma I discussed at the beginning of the chapter, provides a compelling example of this orientation.

At the end of the course, Sarah reexamined her response to the Rifleman's Dilemma and made the following entry in her journal:

Since this will be the last time we turn in our journals, I thought I'd try to look back a little and see how I've changed. What I'd really like to focus on is the morals of war. I remember reading those first handouts . . . [and] the situation I remember best was the rifleman who had to choose whether to kill the woman in the road. At the time I knew very little about Vietnam, and it was hard for me. Now, no more bloodthirsty than I've ever been, I would shoot the woman. I wouldn't be like Goodrich in the war. I would think of my buddies and protect them. It's a risk the woman may be an innocent villager, but the way it was in Vietnam it's a risk you'd have to take. I don't think I would have involved myself in either of the killings in *Fields of Fire* or Caputo's book. These men took justice into their own hands, which even in wartime isn't fair. The line between killing a woman who might very likely be innocent and killing two people who are very likely VC and killed your friends is fine. But . . . killing the VC after the fact without real proof is an act of vengeance. . . .

I guess what I'm saying is the wrong act for the right reason is better than the right act for the wrong reason.

What stands out in this entry is the fact that Sarah can use the incidents she has read about as part of her inquiry into the ethics of killing. Her decision about the dilemma has not changed (she would still shoot the woman), nor have her reasons (she would still do it in order to protect her comrades). But at the end of the course, Sarah can view the rifleman's situation in the context of other acts of killing—those in *A Rumor of War* and *Fields of Fire*. And with that perspective, she can make a "fine" distinction between two cases: the case of killing a woman, even if she turns out to be innocent, when that act has a good chance of protecting her friends ("the wrong act for the right reason"), and the case of killing Vietnamese who are very likely guilty of slaying one's comrades, when that act is purely for revenge ("the right act for the wrong reason"). In short, Sarah demonstrates a sense of moral complexity: right and wrong are not always easy to distinguish, but it is still possible to arrive at reasonable ethical judgments, even in the context of war.

6 Lessons

This course is coming to an end, and while I'm glad to see my last paper in sight, I know that this course has been one of my favorites this semester, if not my favorite. So much is jammed into this course, so many ideas—a semester could go on forever. The literature was excellent, but I especially like the way I was called on to *think*—to look at all the values I have grown up with and ask myself if I want to stick with them. [F/FR/F86]

At the end of each semester, as I read their last journal entries and final reflective essays, I was always struck by the fervor of students' responses to the course. Not all students responded in the same way or claimed to have been affected to the same degree. But most students said that the experience had, in one way or another, changed their attitudes and orientations. For example, Karen expressed a widespread view when she asserted that she had "learned a great deal from this [course], not only about the war itself . . . but also about me—my values, my beliefs, my ideas of right and wrong." A sophomore professed to "have taken a journey from innocence to experience and learned a lot about myself during the semester" [F/SO/S88]. One of the freshmen said that "this class has put me through one hell of a metamorphosis" [M/FR/F89]. And according to a senior:

This is a course which I honestly feel has had a profound effect on my spiritual and intellectual growth. I have never struggled so deeply with such important issues in any other college course. [M/SR/S86]

I was impressed by the sincerity of students' statements about the influence and importance of the Vietnam class. And the course evaluations echoed these sentiments, perhaps even more convincingly, since students wrote them anonymously.[1]

That is not to say that the class transformed students' conceptual orientations or pushed them to higher stages of intellectual and ethical development. I suspect that nothing quite that dramatic happened—or if it did, that it was the exception rather than the rule. Instead, the class introduced students to new complexities of thought and discourse, orienting them to college as a place where reflective judgment would be encouraged and expected. Although a single course could provide only an initiation into these reflective practices, the students seem to have learned several important lessons about the nature of inquiry.

One of those lessons concerned the difference between inquiring into a problem and acquiring facts about it. I remember the stunned look on students' faces when I told them, during an early lecture, that they could put away the notebooks in which many of them were already scribbling: they could put down their pencils because there would be no facts to record and remember, no tests on which to regurgitate information. Students were bemused and bewildered. Was this some sort of hoax? No tests! Was it too good to be true? No notebooks! What was the catch?

The catch was that inquiry would turn out to be the hard road to knowledge, not the easy one—a road pitted with uncertainty and strewn with complexity.

The more I learn about Vietnam, the more confused I become. Why were we there in the first place? How could we let our own countrymen suffer through such conditions? Wasn't anyone thinking? What was going on anyway? . . . Questions. Questions. Questions. [M/FR/F89]

Lessons

Inquiry often led to further questions (rather than settled answers) and to more complicated problems (rather than simple solutions). Sometimes the stream of questions produced frustration, even anxiety. But it also encouraged inquisitiveness and curiosity. As one student noted: "I have always had a curiosity about Vietnam. Now, I'm sorry to say that this curiosity has only increased. I guess this is good, though" [M/FR/F86]. A senior recognized that "instead of answering my questions, I think this course taught me which were the right questions to ask" [F/SR/S86]. And a freshman captured the attitude to inquiry that I tried so hard to foster.

My interest has been held for the last four months like no other course has done, yet I am leaving with more questions than when I came in. . . . There are so many unanswered questions that I am stuck with, but that may be what made this class so good. I am walking out of here knowing more than I knew when I came in, plus I'm anxious to find out more. [M/FR/F86]

In addition, students discovered that significant issues are more often complex than simple, more often contested than settled. As one of the freshmen recognized:

All your life you are brought up in a black and white world, then suddenly you start asking questions and you learn it is not that simple. [F/FR/F89]

Some students were surprised by the complexity and controversy they encountered in a course that purported to be about the Vietnam War in literature. Those who expected to read "war stories" found themselves confronted with challenging texts. And those who expected to find "black and white" issues instead discovered "infinite shades of gray" [F/JR/S86]. For some students, so much uncertainty was disturbing. As a freshman confessed:

153

To be quite honest about it, it has made life a little difficult. I am a person who wants to have no gray areas in my life. I like to know what I think and why. [M/FR/F89]

By the end of the course, however, most of my students seemed to agree with the freshman who said that "things are not all black and white, there are many shades in between. I learned this by the many issues I had to struggle with about Vietnam" [F/FR/F89].

Students struggled especially hard with aesthetic, epistemological, and ethical issues. To encourage literary inquiry, I asked them to read books that challenged their assumptions about good writing and offered alternative modes of representing the war— alternative ways to "tell it." Early in the course, most students were convinced that soldiers' stories offered the truest and best accounts of the Vietnam experience. Then they encountered a series of books that violated their expectations and demanded new strategies of reading and interpretation, especially *Dispatches* and *Going After Cacciato*. Although some students rejected these books as hopelessly obscure or needlessly bizarre, many of my undergraduates recognized that complex texts could represent the war in especially compelling and provocative ways. One of the seniors expressed this sentiment at the end of the semester:

The highlight of the course, for me, was *Dispatches* and *Going After Cacciato*. Before this course began, I probably would have hated both of these books. Something about them, however, attracts me and moves me deeply. They do not answer questions, but make you think about them. [M/SR/S86]

I also wanted students to think about accounts of the past, and here, too, I was more interested in focusing on hard questions than on easy answers. Perhaps the central question was how to know what to believe about events that happened in the past. At the beginning of the course, many students agreed with the senior who said: "I always thought that I could open up a history book, read it, and understand what the Vietnam War

was like" [M/SR/S86]. However, the unit on the Hué Massacre
opened many students' eyes to the fact that there can be different
"histories" of an event, each based on claims and facts and expert
opinions. By the end of the course, students began to treat all
accounts with a healthy skepticism, using comparative and evaluative analysis to decide which version of an event to believe.

I have realized that not all history is simply black and white.
Before working with the Hué material, I believed that everything
I read about the Vietnam War was true—cut and dry. If someone
said it, I believed it. I now have come to see, especially through
the Hué articles, that I was dead wrong. [M/FR/F86]

Reflective thinking is also central to ethical inquiry, although
some students wondered, initially, whether moral reflection had
any place in war. As one student expressed this logic: "Things
that went on weren't right, but then what is war? War doesn't
make sense, so how can we make sense out of war?" [F/FR/F89].
In war, soldiers seem to be free from the codes that bind them in
peacetime; in war, therefore, anything goes. But when students
found out what "anything" can include, they conceded that not
all killing was equally justifiable, even in war, and that a combat
zone must not be placed off-limits to moral assessment and
ethical judgment. Nevertheless, students also recognized that
the circumstances of war complicate moral reflection, so that
soldiers' actions require careful and compassionate deliberation.
One of the freshmen summed up her experience with ethical
inquiry in this way:

Before I started reading the material, I thought I knew right from
wrong. I had always been taught that something either is or it
isn't; it can't be both. I know now, more often than not, that
decisions are very complex, and there isn't one right or wrong
answer. . . . At the beginning, things were always back and
white for me, but now and in the readings, everything is gray.
. . . I am not so quick to judge people now. I can realize the
complexity of problems. [F/FR/F86]

Finally, the course taught students that inquiry can be connected as well as critical, responsive as well as reflective, an activity of heart as well as mind. Most students found ways to forge empathetic and emotional connections to the war, sometimes even profound and personal connections. But connected inquiry provided no easy or certain path to knowledge, and students soon learned that it could be difficult to build bridges between heartfelt response and critical reflection. For example, when they read the memoirs by Caputo and Van Devanter, students struggled to balance emotion and reason, sympathy and skepticism—the dissonant voices in their hearts and their heads. As one freshman discovered: "Finding a balance between critical and compassionate thinking is difficult" [F/FR/F89].

Although I saw convincing evidence that students were able to engage in reflective inquiry during the semester, I always wondered whether my course had made a deep and lasting impression on them. Students were, to be sure, enthusiastic in their evaluations of the course. But how would the lessons of connected and critical thinking fare in other courses and other spheres of life? I remember being especially concerned about this question at the end of my first semester of teaching the Vietnam course to a large class of freshmen. Because I'd developed a special relationship with these students, I was especially sad to see them depart, suspecting that I would lose contact with most of them. In another month the students were caught up in the turmoil of a new semester. And so was I. A year passed, then two. I lost track of most of them.

There were occasions, however, when I crossed paths with students from that first freshman course, often when they were sophomores or juniors. Even in brief conversations, typically on the way to class, they made a point of saying that some things from the Vietnam course had stuck with them. Perhaps they were only being courteous. But their statements went beyond what was required by kindness, and I detected conviction, sometimes even passion, in their voices. The more of these brief conversations I had, the more I wanted to explore what students remembered from that class their freshman year.

In the spring of 1990, with this book project nearing completion, I realized that those freshmen were seniors, and that many of them would graduate shortly. If I wanted to talk with them, I had one last opportunity. Time was short and my plan was modest: I would interview half of the twenty-six freshmen whose journals I had photocopied in 1986. I chose nine women and four men whose work suggested that they had been committed to the course and engaged by the issues it raised. When I tried to track them down, I discovered that two of the women had transferred to universities in other states and that one of the men was pursuing an internship in a nearby city. Nevertheless, I was able to arrange hour-long interviews with all thirteen students during March and early April 1990.

I began the interviews with an open-ended question: after nearly four years, what stood out in their minds when they thought back on the Vietnam course?[2] That broad question elicited a variety of responses. Some students recalled how hard they had worked that first semester of college. One young man was particularly forthright in his views.

Actually, as I was going through the course, you know, it seemed like a pain, just about like every other course seemed like a pain.

Especially painful was the Hué assignment, which this student described as "just a monster of an assignment." He elaborated:

I mean, it was hard, really hard. I mean you could work on that forever, with the information given, and you would never know if you were right or wrong. . . . Yeah, I remember that. I worked very diligently on that.

But looking back on the course as a senior, he remembered it with affection and appreciation.

Now some of the readings were very dry, I thought, but for the most part I enjoyed doing the work for the class, more so than other classes. Now, as I remember the course now, I remember it as one of my favorite courses that I've had in college. So it kind of grows on you, I think. I think the course was really a productive course. I mean, while you're taking a course it's hard to—you're kind of right down in the micro level, and you can't really see how good or how bad it is until you look back on it.

Looking back four years later, several students mentioned their journal writing as one of the most significant components of the course. Some of them said that they still had their journals, and a few even reported having looked through them before coming for the interview.

Last night, even, I was looking through all this—I still have all my stuff from the class—and I was kinda looking through my journal. And that journal was the best thing. . . . because I put down like my feelings on things.

One woman remarked that the journal had been particularly important to her because, as a freshman, she was shy about expressing her views orally.

I enjoyed writing the journal. I remember at the time I thought it was a lot of writing, but looking back I thought that it was a really good thing to do. So if you're teaching it again, I'd say that was a strong point, that was a good time to reflect on the issues and stuff. . . . I'm not a real verbal person, like in class, but I enjoy writing down my thoughts, in like a journal. And I think that really helps a person that's not verbal, to be able to express themselves.

Another student, who had also dug out her journal before our meeting, was amused by how much emotion was revealed in her entries. But she recognized that when she had responded personally and passionately to issues and ideas, they remained with her after the course was over.

Lessons

I went through my file for the course and . . . I read through my journal. It was kind of interesting. It seemed like with some of the things that I wrote, I said the same things like every other day. I wrote, "Well, this really disturbed me" or "This kind of upset me." You know, I kind of laugh at myself now. But all the things, I mean a lot of the things, stuck with me, I think, because they were so personal, you know. . . . Some of the accounts, like *Born on the Fourth of July* and *Home Before Morning*—it's just more personal, and I guess it clicks more when I can relate to it.

However, the kind of connected inquiry that the journal writing fostered was not often encouraged in subsequent courses—at least not according to these students' reports. Their experiences seem to confirm recent judgments that personal and emotional ways of knowing are typically "banished" from college classrooms, where the "public, rational, analytical voice" is alone accorded "tutelage, respect, and rewards" (Belenky et al. 124). Thus one of the ways in which students remembered my course as "different" was, not surprisingly, in its endorsement of emotional response, personal writing, and heartfelt involvement as acceptable modes of inquiry. And one student was especially struck by how unusual it was for a teacher to be so connected with a course.

I've never seen a teacher who was upset or who got emotionally involved in a class. I still haven't had one that got emotionally involved in a class, since I had you.

In other cases, students remembered the course mainly as an experience that opened their eyes to hard questions and difficult issues.

We're coming out of, you know, suburbia, middle-class . . . and then all of a sudden one day you give us this stuff. And we're like, wait a minute, I just got out of graduation and prom, what is the deal?! I mean obviously, it was like—wow, this is pretty heavy stuff! So I was being bombarded with all these really big questions.

For some, the "heavy stuff" encouraged an attitude of reflective skepticism, making them wary of accepting any single view as authoritative. One student claimed that the course had taught her to look for alternative perspectives.

One of the things I thought the course did really well was show how, you know, you can never get a full side of the story until you look at all the different points of view, and how one person sees something totally different than another person does.

Another commented on how surprised she was, at the beginning of the course, to find the discrepant accounts of the Battle of Ap Bac.

Like when I read these articles [about Ap Bac] I thought, man [laughs], these two accounts, I thought, phew, you never know what these articles are telling you!

Yet another student answered my question about what "stood out" in her memory by mentioning the Hué unit.

The best thing I remember is the paper we wrote on the battle of Hué. Because that was just so wild for me to see all these different accounts and not know what really happened. I mean, because it was such a—I mean, I guess I never realized how nobody knew what was going on.

When I probed for more information, she explained why it was so significant that she could adopt a critical, questioning attitude.

See, I never had to question anything, because it was just there. It's not that my parents didn't ever have me question anything, it's just that I never really thought about it. And so I was just so trusting of other people, I guess, that I just believed everything. And that's something that's totally changed. I mean your class, having it freshman semester really opened my eyes to that—not to believe everything.

Lessons

Because I was interested in whether other college courses had encouraged the kind of reflective inquiry I tried to foster, I asked students to tell me about their experiences with ethical and critical thinking. They had relatively little to say about ethical reflection. One student mentioned that she had taken a class on professional ethics (in journalism), and only one other—a woman who was preparing for a career in physical rehabilitation—said that she had considered questions of ethics and values in her courses: "I mean there's always issues in the classes about what's right and what's wrong, especially when dealing with a lot of disabilities." Apparently, ethical reflection was not a salient feature of most of these students' college experience.

However, all of the students I interviewed, irrespective of major or field of study, talked convincingly about the ways in which their college courses had encouraged them to be more skeptical, analytical, and critical in their quest for knowledge. In several cases, this critical orientation seems to have grown out of the recognition that experts disagree and opinions vary, even on important matters. As one student said about her history courses:

And the books we've read are from different points of view. They're not just all thinking the same way. Well, this one contradicts this one. You know. And I think that the way that I've changed—you know, with my analytical skills or whatever—I think that probably has to do with just taking classes.

Not surprisingly, the classes that seem to have had the greatest impact on students' awareness of intellectual complexity were advanced courses in their fields of study. For example, a psychology major claimed that his courses typically included different explanations for the same phenomena.

Opposing viewpoints or theories—yeah, I get that in psychology all the time. You're going—well, "I have this theory that this function of mine is how this works," and someone else goes, "No, I have this theory," and it's like—then you have someone that comes up and combines the two—and like "I have this eclectic theory here."

An American Studies major talked about how a seminar had recently introduced her to complexities of interpretation in the study of history and culture.

How do we interpret what happened and how do we make it real? Like how do we know what really happened? . . . And you can't dissect history and find an answer the same way you can in the hard sciences, you just can't. So what we have to do is, you have to go through this process of like interpretation, which . . . we're just starting to figure out.

And a criminal justice student compared what she first encountered in the Hué unit to an experience she had in a later course.

It makes me wonder, like, when you read a history book how much of that's true, and how much is—well . . . I did read, in one of my criminal justice classes, *A People's History of the United States,* and all this about Columbus killing all these people, and I thought, man I've never read *this* before [laughs]. And I thought, God, I've never even *heard* this perspective about how he killed all these people when he came over here, and exploited them. And I thought: the things that they keep from you!

But classes were not the only influence on students' critical thinking: I heard an intriguing story from the student who was working on a school-sponsored internship with a government agency. His job involved handling complaints about employment practices, a task that showed him how easily the facts could be manipulated to serve particular interests. That recognition confirmed his skepticism about accepting a single version of any event as "the truth."

So, you know, I'm becoming more skeptical. I hope so, anyway. I have to be. When you get the story from the charging party, it's very unsophisticated. . . . And then the lawyers' [versions] are spiffy, and they've got everything detailed just the way you want to see it. . . . So it's easier to lean toward that side, but you've got to really try to be skeptical. So I hope I'm more like that.

Obviously, these thirteen students remembered different aspects of the Vietnam course when they recalled their experiences as freshmen. They were, nevertheless, in broad agreement about the significance of the class, and many of them cited the personal or emotional aspects of the course, or what I have called connected inquiry, as the dimension that remained most salient in their memories. For example, one woman talked about finding a "certain level of intensity that people don't count on—that takes you by surprise." This student—I'll call her Ann—recalled how eagerly she had looked forward to coming to college and taking a class that promised to engage both her heart and her mind.

My mom and I were driving down to register [for freshman year], and I read through that whole course list and guide. And there was one course about the Vietnam War, and it had this emotional, possibly, or more just social aspect or something—this *issue*, you know, there's an issue here and you're going to be involved with it. And that was really thrilling for me. I was really looking for that. Maybe not even consciously. . . . It was a *problem*, you know, the problem aspect really enticed me.

Throughout the course, Ann became increasingly connected, emotionally, with the war and the soldiers' experiences. At times, she even saw those experiences as a metaphor for her own struggles as a college freshman: the soldiers became symbols of the human capacity to endure hardship and adversity.

And it was comforting for me to know that those people had gone through all that. I almost liked them—no, I *did* like them. I felt very close to them. . . . I'm just saying that I did feel a certain connection to their experience.

However, that intense connection also created a problem for Ann: how would she cope when she moved on to other courses and other topics that did not elicit the same intensity and emotional involvement?

One thing I do remember was, second semester coming back. And the first week feeling very let down. Almost disappointed, like I don't really want to be here, I have no purpose, like there's nothing gripping any more. Like this is silly stuff, you know?

Fortunately, Ann soon had a cathartic experience; it happened when she went to see the film *Platoon* that winter.

And then walking to the movies and seeing *Platoon*. And walking out and thinking, "I'm so relieved that I don't have to think about that any more." It's like, "I'm so glad that's over with. I thought about that so much, and I don't have to think about it any more." It's like, "OK, then leave it." And that was good.

Freed from the spell of the course, Ann began to view its effects more reflectively. As a senior, she could look back on her freshman experience with critical perspective. At several points in our conversation, Ann revealed she was aware that the Vietnam course had been so powerful because she had experienced it at a particular stage in her intellectual and emotional life.

Yeah, I mean, it really affected me, there's no question about it. I now have had an experience where a course affected me more so, but at the same time, at the stage where I was then, you know, that was probably a pretty high—a pretty big effect.

And Ann also indicated that she would probably respond differently to a Vietnam course now, at this later stage in her intellectual development. For example, she mentioned that a friend was currently taking a class on the war literature, prompting Ann to speculate about how she would respond if she were in that course.

Now, I think when I hear about the class my friend is taking . . . I think I would have probably experienced it more on a detached, objective—[as a] social issue. I don't know why. . . . [In a freshman course] you're first stepping into college, maybe [that] has something to do with it, or the fact that chronologically that course came right after a lot of things.

Of the students I interviewed, Ann had one of the most complex, and possibly one of the most conflicted, responses to the course. Sometimes she was nostalgic about her freshman experience, longing to recapture the depth of her felt responses and the intensity of her emotional and personal connections. At other times, she seemed embarrassed that she had responded emotionally, rather than dispassionately and critically, to the war and its literature. Ann seemed uncertain how to integrate the disparate responses in her heart and her mind.[3]

I hoped that the interviews would give me a better sense of how my course was remembered and whether any of its impact had endured through four years of college. Although my small-scale project can only be suggestive, there were clear indications that these students still, even at the end of their undergraduate experience, viewed the Vietnam course as an emotionally powerful and intellectually challenging experience, and that the lessons of critical inquiry, at least, had been nurtured in subsequent courses. Their responses were encouraging.

I was also encouraged by the responses of students from the smaller versions of the course, including some of the upperclassmen who graduated when the semester ended. Although I lost track of most of them, some kept in touch, usually by dropping a note a year or more later. Their comments— unsolicited and unexpected—confirmed my impression that the effects of the course did not disappear when the semester ended. For example, a senior in my first course (spring 1986) wrote from graduate school on the West Coast in September 1988, urging me to keep teaching the class.

Hope you're still teaching the Vietnam class. I feel it was one of the most important courses I had. And not just because it dealt with the Vietnam War. Rather, your course taught something all college courses should, but for the most part don't strive for: how to think. By coping, discussing, and trying to come to terms with many difficult, thought-provoking, and largely unanswerable issues, I learned more in your class than I did in many other classes combined.

And two-and-a-half years after he finished my course, another student wrote to say that he had finished a master's degree at an Ivy League university and qualified for training for the foreign service corps.

I am convinced that your class on the Vietnam War influenced and reinforced my decision to pursue a career in diplomacy. I want to work to *avoid wars*, to work for peace. I think your class also helped me to realize what some of the traps are that I will face—ideology, misunderstanding, biases, extremism, subjective officials, ignorance, misinformation, etc. Your class has really prepared me, and I think some of the ideas and questions you planted will make me a better diplomat and a better person. I will never forget the class—I think it was the best and most significant course I ever took.

A "significant course": each time I teach it, I try to provide such a course for my students. When I got off that plane in Oakland in July 1970, I never imagined that I would teach a class about the Vietnam War, an experience I was determined to put behind me. As a soldier, I had seen firsthand the hollow rhetoric of that slogan about winning "hearts and minds." As a teacher, I have tried to reclaim and redeem that phrase, using it to describe a course that fosters personal connection and critical reflection—a course that stirs students' hearts and challenges their minds.

Appendixes
Notes
Works Cited
Index

Appendix A:
The Battle
of Ap Bac

In the early years of the Vietnam War most of the fighting in South Vietnam consisted of skirmishes between two factions. One faction was the Army of the Republic of Vietnam (the ARVN). The ARVN forces were loyal to the South Vietnamese government. The other faction was the Viet Cong (or VC), a guerrilla army opposed to the established government.

One of the first major battles between ARVN and VC forces occurred on January 2, 1963, when South Vietnamese intelligence reported a VC radio station operating near the village of Ap Bac. A large number of ARVN troops, with American military advisors, converged on the village in an effort to engage the small VC force that was supposed to be guarding the station.

However, accounts of what happened at Ap Bac—and what these events meant—differ. On the following pages you will find two historical accounts of the ARVN operation at Ap Bac, both based on documented reports from participants, observers, and military analysts.

Account 1

At the battle of Ap Bac, the ARVN 7th Infantry Division went after the battle-tested 514th Viet Cong battalion, about five-hundred soldiers, including specialists in antiaircraft and antitank tactics.[1] Although the ARVN had a well-conceived plan of attack, they had received poor intelligence information and therefore

169

misjudged the size and location of the VC force. The VC, on the other hand, had learned the details of the coming attack from their spies.[2] With this advanced warning, the VC were able to pick the ground they wanted to fight on. They were dug into positions along a canal and tree line, giving them excellent protection and concealment, as well as a murderous line of fire on anything that tried to cross the open rice fields in front of them.

The ARVN engaged the VC unit, but the attack against the well-fortified VC quickly bogged down. The ARVN lost some helicopters and light tanks, and were unable to advance to the VC fortifications before nightfall. But that night, under the cover of darkness, the VC fled from their positions. The next morning the ARVN forces took control of Ap Bac.

The VC lost perhaps fifty or more killed and an unknown number of wounded; ARVN casualities were about sixty killed and one hundred wounded.[3] Thus, in terms of casualties, some military analysts (such as Colonel D. R. Palmer) felt the battle had been "a draw."[4] Nevertheless, the ARVN achieved their objective at Ap Bac: they forced the VC to retreat from the village. Thus the American high command viewed the battle as an ARVN triumph, and a sign that the South Vietnamese army could acomplish its missions. General Paul Harkins, head of the U.S. military command in South Vietnam, called Ap Bac a "victory" for the ARVN.[5] And the ARVN Corps Commander, General Cao, announced that the battle was "a victory that laid the foundation for our success. . . . Ap Bac is a symbol of the South Vietnamese people's will to resist."[6]

NOTES

1. Dave Richard Palmer, *Summons of the Trumpet: A History of the Vietnam War from a Military Man's Viewpoint* (New York: Ballantine Books, 1978), 44.

2. Kuno Knoebl, *Victor Charlie* (New York: Praeger, 1967), 84.

3. Palmer, 50.

4. Palmer, 50.

5. David Halberstam, *The Making of a Quagmire* (New York: Random House, 1965), 156; Knoebl, 91.

6. Quoted in Knoebl, 81.

Account 2

At the battle of Ap Bac, a vastly superior ARVN force of over three thousand soldiers, most of them from the crack Seventh Infantry Division, went after two companies of Viet Cong (about two hundred forty soldiers) reinforced with about fifty local guerrillas.[1] Even with this ten to one advantage, with American advisors, and with vastly superior firepower (including bombers, artillery, helicopters, and armored vehicles), the ARVN were unable to overrun the VC unit, which was armed with only four machine guns, some automatic rifles, and carbines.

The ARVN attacked at dawn, but the assault went badly. As soon as they took casualties, the ARVN troops panicked and refused to advance. When ten helicopters tried to land more soldiers, five of the aircraft were destroyed and four others damaged by VC machine-gun fire. And when the ARVN armored vehicles attempted to advance, a VC squad of fifteen men destroyed four of the tanks and damaged two others, stopping the assault.[2] After a full day of fighting, the VC were still secure in their positions, having taken very few casualties. Under the cover of darkness, the VC unit escaped from the ARVN "trap."

ARVN losses were heavy (sixty-one killed and about one hundred wounded) compared to VC losses (three bodies left on the battlefield and losses estimated at no more than twelve).[3] It seems clear that the ARVN had performed badly in the fight. Even the senior U.S. Army advisor to the ARVN division, Lieutenant Colonel John P. Vann, called the ARVN attack on Ap Bac "a miserable damn performance."[4] French journalist Bernard Fall called the battle "disastrous," a "humiliating defeat" for the ARVN.[5] For the VC, on the other hand, this first major battle provided a new confidence that their small guerrilla units could repulse much larger forces armed with superior weapons. Thus Australian war correspondent Wilfred Burchett proclaimed the battle a "turning point" in the war, since it gave the VC a psychological advantage and won new recruits to its cause.[6]

NOTES

1. Wilfred G. Burchett, *Vietnam: Inside Story of the Guerilla War* (New York: International Publishers, 1965), 88; Kuno Knoebl, *Victor Charlie* (New York: Praeger, 1967), 84.

2. Knoebl, 86.

3. Stanley Karnow, *Vietnam: A History* (New York: Viking Press, 1983), 262; Terrence Maitland and Stephen Weiss, *The Vietnam Experience: Raising the Stakes* (Boston: Boston Publishing, 1982), 51.

4. Maitland and Weiss, 51.

5. Bernard B. Fall, introduction to Knoebl, xii.

6. Burchett, 88.

Questions

1. When historical accounts of the same event are different, can you believe one of the accounts more than another? Why?

2. Is either of these accounts more likely to be true? Please explain your answer.

3. What really happened at Ap Bac? Why do you think so?

Appendix B:
The Rifleman's
Dilemma

During the Vietnam War, an infantry squad was patrolling deep in enemy-controlled territory. At one point in this operation, the squad leader decided to scout along a trail that ran through a valley, leading toward a village a short distance away. The squad leader told one of his riflemen, a private named Johnson, to stay on a small hilltop as a lookout, while the rest of the squad went along the trail in the valley below.

As Johnson was watching the squad make its way along the trail, he noticed a Vietnamese woman appear on the trail just ahead of the squad, but around a bend so that they could not see her. The woman leaned over at the edge of the trail and then quickly moved back into the underbrush—out of sight of the squad, but still visible to Johnson.

Johnson was immediately suspicious. This was enemy-controlled territory, and the woman could easily be part of the local guerrilla forces. On the other hand, many innocent peasants lived in and around the villages. Was the woman a guerrilla soldier who might set off a mine or booby trap when the squad came around the bend in the trail? Or was the woman simply a peasant who had perhaps dropped something on the trail in her haste to hide from the advancing American soldiers?

As these thoughts went through Johnson's mind, the squad kept moving and now was almost at the spot where the woman was hiding. The squad was too far away for Johnson to call out to them. Even a warning shot would probably not stop them from proceeding around the bend. Johnson raised his rifle and lined up his sights on the woman in the brush. But as his finger tightened on the trigger, he hesitated.

If he shot the woman and there turned out not to be a booby trap on the trail, he would have murdered an innocent person. But if he didn't shoot her, a number of his friends might be blown to bits if the woman detonated a mine.

Questions

What should Private Johnson do: hold his fire or shoot the woman? Why is that the right thing for him to do?

Appendix C:
List Of
Course Texts

Note: Semesters in Brackets

Broyles, William, Jr. *Brothers in Arms: A Journey from War to Peace.*
New York: Avon, 1986. [F89]
Caputo, Philip. *A Rumor of War.* New York: Ballantine, 1977.
[S86, F86, S88, F89]
Herr, Michael. *Dispatches.* New York: Avon, 1968. [S86, F86, S88,
F89]
Komunyakaa, Yusef. *Dien Cai Dau.* Middletown: Wesleyan UP,
1988. [F89]
Kovic, Ron. *Born on the Fourth of July.* New York: Pocket Books,
1976. [F86]
O'Brien, Tim. *Going After Cacciato.* New York: Dell, 1975. [S86,
F86, S88, F89]
Santoli, Al. *Everything We Had.* New York: Ballantine, 1981. [S86,
F86, S88, F89]
Van Devanter, Lynda. *Home Before Morning.* New York: Warner,
1983. [S86, F86, S88, F89]
Webb, James. *Fields of Fire.* New York: Bantam, 1978. [S86, S88]

Notes

1. Reading, Writing, and . . . Vietnam?

1. For comprehensive lists of books about the war see Newman or Wittman.

2. Courses on the war have proliferated in the last decade. *Newsweek* featured some of them in an article entitled "The Classroom Vietnam War." Others are discussed by Franklin. Some courses attempt to integrate history and literature by arranging the readings according to the chronology of the war (see Ehrhart). My course was most similar to courses that focus on the literature of the war rather than on history or politics (see, for example, Christie, Enders, Olham). However, literary issues provided only one strand of inquiry in my course.

3. The phrase "hearts and minds" was used to describe the goals of the counterinsurgency (or "pacification") program in Vietnam. This program was based on what Summers describes as the "premise that the key to winning the war was to win the allegiance of the Vietnamese people" (188). When I arrived in Vietnam in the summer of 1969, everyone I met treated the phrase as a joke. No one cared what happened to the Vietnamese; we all just wanted to survive the year and go home. Maclear notes that the Marines had a slogan which summed up the grunts' attitude: "Get 'em by the balls and their hearts and minds will follow" (255).

4. Most of the students who took my courses did so to fulfill requirements. For freshmen, my courses met the basic composition requirement, and for upperclassmen they fulfilled an inten-

sive-writing requirement for the College of Arts and Sciences. As a result, students were eager to get a seat in my classes, and in some cases they were so desperate that they registered without knowing what the course would be about. To be sure, some students knew that my class was going to be about the literature of the Vietnam War, and a number of them enrolled because of their interest in the topic. But in all too many cases, students were more interested in fulfilling their writing requirement than in learning about Vietnam. One of the students in my course for upperclassmen confessed: "I'm taking this course to fulfill my intensive writing requirement—I didn't know the course topic until the first day." And when I asked my freshmen why they were taking this particular course, I read numerous statements like the following: "To be honest, the first English class I signed up for was one that dealt with tragedies, but it was already full. I signed up for this one because it was one of the few that were left; I didn't have any idea what subjects it was going to deal with."

5. The situation in high school may be changing. For example, there is now a high-school social-studies curriculum for teaching about the war; see Starr, *The Lessons of the Vietnam War* and "The Making of *The Lessons of the Vietnam War*."

6. In the smaller versions of the course I also asked students to participate in two projects as part of their orientation to the war. For the first, I selected a dozen photographs of key events, ranging from the battle of Dienbienphu to the exodus of the boat people. I put students into groups of two or three, assigning one of the pictures to each group. The group's task was to identify the event depicted and to give a brief report about what happened and why it was significant. Students used a set of history texts, magazines, and books of photographs, all on reserve in the library. At the end of the students' reports, I gave a short lecture on the history of American involvement in Vietnam, filling in the connections between the key events depicted in the photographs. For the second project, students used a series of

maps to determine what a soldier's experience would have been like in a particular area of South Vietnam. Students again worked in teams to produce reports on the area they were assigned.

7. I collected these notebooks five times during the semester, writing comments in the margins and awarding points for meeting my criteria—regular, detailed, thoughtful, and honest writing. I gave a maximum of three points each time I collected the journals, so that the journals comprised 15 percent of the grade for the course.

8. I did not select these journals in a systematic or scientific way. I tended to copy those that were full and interesting, so that my sample probably over-represents the work of those students who took the journal writing most seriously. But in truth, nearly all of the students in my courses were quite conscientious about writing in their journals, so that at the end of every semester I had an abundance of full and intriguing journals to choose from. My sample contains thirty-three journals from men and thirty-seven from women. Because I taught mostly freshmen, the largest number of journals (forty-seven) are from first-year students. I collected two journals from sophomores, nine from juniors, and eighteen from seniors.

9. In reprinting the excerpts, I corrected some spelling mistakes and punctuation errors, but otherwise the entries are exactly as they appeared in the students' journals. In order to keep excerpts brief, I often deleted redundancies and irrelevancies, but I always marked those deletions with ellipses.

10. I elaborate on this point in my essay "Observing Students' Reflective Thinking."

11. When I speak of a "broadly conceived pragmatist orientation," I am referring specifically to several educational theorists in that tradition who have had a major influence on my work, especially Kitchener, "Educational Goals," Perry, *Intellectual and Ethical Development* and "Cognitive and Ethical Growth," and Rosenblatt, *Literature as Exploration*. However, the key source for my ideas about "reflective inquiry" is Dewey's *How We Think*.

12. In my classes, I referred to the journal as a "logbook," in part to distinguish it from the kind of personal journals or diaries that students may have kept in the past. However, throughout this book I use the term "journal" consistently, and so I've substituted that term for the word "logbook" when it appeared in excerpts from students' writing.

2. Connected Inquiry

1. My emphasis on personal response was based on the conviction that engaged reading will, in Louise Rosenblatt's words, "necessarily involve the sensuous and emotional responsiveness, the human sympathies, of the reader" (*Literature as Exploration* 52). Moreover, feelings can be central to understanding. For example, in *Women's Ways of Knowing*, Mary Field Belenky and her colleagues argue that feelings, emotions, empathy, personal experience, heartfelt response, and subjective engagement play a significant role in the process of learning and knowing. See also Nussbaum. Although I devoted a good deal of energy to fostering the analytical voices of my students, I tried not to ignore their empathetic voices or to banish emotions from my classes.

2. The term "connected" comes from Belenky et al. Their concept of "connected knowing" is closely related to what I call "connected inquiry." However, I have drawn most heavily on Rosenblatt, especially *Literature as Exploration*, to develop my ideas about connected inquiry.

3. The authors of *Women's Ways of Knowing* argue that opportunities for personal involvement and connected knowing are especially important for college women, because they often feel trapped in an analytical mode that doesn't allow room for emotive or intuitive responses. Although such broad generalizations inevitably oversimplify, my students' responses did tend to divide along gender lines. Moreover, I found a few instances in

which women said that they felt alienated from analysis and attracted to opportunities to engage in personal response.

4. Students' efforts to identify with the soldiers were facilitated, I suspect, by the fact that the troops in Vietnam were so young, about the age of the freshmen in my classes.

How many times did I stop reading and realize that he was my age? I see myself laying in the jungle waiting for morning to break. My God, what would I have done? . . . It scares the shit out of me to think that I might have gone. [M/FR/F89]

The average age of the American Vietnam soldier was *nineteen*. I'd heard this before and I realized that this was very young, but several things put this in perspective for me today. For one, I'll be nineteen in just three months. I realized this today. I'm the same age as the soldiers that fought in Vietnam. These "men" were my age. [M/FR/F89]

5. The most successful method was to get students to talk with Vietnamese men and women who had memories of the war. That happened occasionally in my courses, and when it did it produced powerful responses. I always showed some videotapes in which Vietnamese (from both North and South) talked about their experiences of the war. And some students took on independent projects in which they read memoirs by Vietnamese, like those by Hayslip or Ngoc. But because my course focused on books about the American experience in Vietnam, the Vietnamese perspective was inevitably shortchanged and perhaps distorted.

6. From June 1969 to January 1970, I was a platoon leader with the 446th Transportation Company (Medium Truck). From January to June 1970, I was a staff officer (S–1) at 6th Transportation Battalion headquarters.

7. More than a year later, Karen was still working on making connections with her father's war experiences. I received the following letter from her late in January 1991: "Over the last two weeks I have been falling back on my experiences in your course.

The war in the Gulf has sparked my father into talking to me about his time in Vietnam. And I don't think I would have been as well prepared to listen if it were not for everything you made me think about that semester. Although I do not have my journal with me, I try to remember all the questions I had then, and I actually feel able—and comfortable—asking him them now. My father and I have never been closer, and I thank *you* in part for that."

3. Literary Inquiry

1. For recent assessments of the importance and influence of Rosenblatt's work, see the essays in Clifford and in Farrell and Squire. My approach to literary inquiry was also similar to Booth's concept of "coduction."

2. I understood that reluctance to "criticize" better when I asked one of my classes to read Ron Kovic's *Born on the Fourth of July* at the end of the semester. Kovic's book is a personal account in the same tradition as the memoirs by Caputo and Van Devanter, though closer to Van Devanter in its emotional style and confessional approach. But at the end of the course, students were divided about how well this emotional approach worked. Although some praised Kovic's book for its intensity, others found that the emotional approach no longer seemed as viable as it had earlier in the year, when they were reading *Home Before Morning*. For some, Kovic had pushed techniques of intensity "too far." Why were these freshmen able to bring their critical judgment to bear on Kovic's intensely personal account? For at least some of them, critical reflection became possible when they recognized that they could critique a way of representing an experience without criticizing the integrity of the person involved. In other words, these students discovered that they could respond with wholehearted sympathy to Kovic as a human being and at the same time recognize flaws in the way he told his story. One of the students said it well: "I think what is really

in question here is the *book* not the *person*—I really feel terribly for Kovic, but that doesn't mean that I have to adore the WAY he tells his story" [F/FR/F86].

3. My own judgments were mostly on the side of the minority: in my view, Caputo's book is both better written and more thought-provoking than Van Devanter's. I did not hide those judgments from students, but I never argued forcefully for them, either. Rather, I tried to create a classroom in which a range of views could be voiced and examined, and where reasonable people could arrive at different judgments about literary texts.

4. My understanding of *Dispatches* owes a great deal to John Hellman's analysis of Herr as a "new journalist." See *Fables of Fact*, chapter 6.

5. Although I agreed with many of the students' judgments, I also recognized that they were harsh on Webb because they read his novel late in the course, when they were already familiar with the issues and plots of the Vietnam story, and also because they read *Fields of Fire* immediately after one of the finest books to come out of the war—*Dispatches*. Moreover, *Fields* provided important material for ethical inquiry, as I will discuss in chapter 5.

4. Critical Inquiry

1. There are, broadly speaking, two different ways to conceive of "critical reflection," and although they are not necessarily incompatible, these two approaches often lead to different orientations and practices. One approach is primarily socio-political, fostering a critical orientation to one's culture and encouraging "ideological suspicion" in students. The work of Shor and Giroux illustrate this first approach. The other approach to "critical reflection" is primarily conceptual, fostering a critical orientation to knowledge and encouraging "epistemological suspicion," or what I prefer to call "reflective skepticism." I take this to be

Dewey's approach in *How We Think*, and it is also illustrated in Paul (*Critical Thinking*) and Siegel. From the perspective of the first approach, my course failed to foster truly "critical" reflection, since students did not interrogate the political-cultural-ideological matrix from which the war emerged and within which it has been represented. Because my project was rooted in the second orientation to reflective thinking, however, the focus of the course was to encourage inquiry into epistemological and ethical issues.

2. William Broyles makes this point in "Why Men Love War" when he comments on a particularly cryptic story: "Its purpose is not to enlighten but to exclude; its message is not its content but putting the listener in his place. I suffered, I was there. You were not" (61).

3. In a recent assessment of the battle, Kirkpatrick concludes: "It was, from beginning to end, a Communist victory" ("Decision" 53).

4. For details of these models, see Perry, *Intellectual and Ethical Development* and "Cognitive and Ethical Growth"; Kitchener, "Educational Goals" and "Reflective Judgment Model"; and Kitchener and King, "Concepts of Justification" and "Transforming Assumptions."

5. For Perry, relativism—although a powerful mode of thinking—can become an intellectual game, leading to countless judgments from multiple perspectives, but no real decisions. As Perry puts it, "reason alone will leave the thinker with several legitimate contexts and no way of choosing among them" (*Intellectual and Ethical Development* 135). The solution, then, is to transcend reason, while still honoring it, by making a thoughtful affirmation. This leads to the final position in Perry's scheme, "Commitment in Relativism," as students work out responsible choices and make commitments to careers and life projects.

6. Studies with the Reflective Judgment interview indicate that most beginning college students tend to make judgments on the basis of intuitions, feelings, and personal beliefs, while upper-

classmen are typically "practical skeptics," convinced that beliefs are matters of opinion but also aware that evidence has some bearing on judgments of competing claims. Moreover, this research suggests that very few college students become "probabilists." See Kitchener, "Reflective Judgment Model."

7. I also did not adopt some other assumptions and methods of a strictly developmental approach. In contrast to the developmental models, I assumed that critical inquiry (by which I mean analytical, comparative, and evaluative thinking) was within the grasp of most college students—not habitually, perhaps, and not in all conditions and circumstances, but in at least some contexts and with respect to certain kinds of problems. As Richard Paul has said: "The ability to think critically is a matter of *degree*. No one is without *any* critical skills, and no one has them . . . fully" ("Critical Thinking" 7). Therefore, I was optimistic that I could engage many of my students—even college freshmen—in critical inquiry. That optimism contrasts with the views of Kitchener and King: "It is unlikely that young adults, even given the best educational environment, will very often use the kind of reflective judgment that Dewey idealized" ("Transforming Assumptions" 174).

8. The officer was John Paul Vann, about whom much has been written recently. See especially Sheehan.

9. Bernard Fall was not only a highly regarded journalist but an eminent Vietnam scholar, the author of a series of important books on the French and American military involvement in Indochina. Fall was born in Vienna (1926) but raised and educated in France. He came to the United States in 1950, on a Fulbright grant, and stayed to earn his doctorate at Syracuse University. Fall retained his French citizenship, however. He wrote prolifically about the situation in Vietnam, conducting research in the field. He was killed by a mine while on patrol with the Marines in February 1967. For an informative profile, see Kirkpatrick, "Bernard Fall." Wilfred Burchett, an Australian journalist, was a

self-proclaimed Communist and a supporter of the North Vietnamese/Viet Cong cause.

10. In fall 1986, 31 percent of the students could not choose one of the accounts as more likely to be true; in fall 1989, 23 percent could not decide on an account.

11. In 1986, 44 percent of the students chose Account 2; in 1989, 48 percent did so. (By contrast, 25 percent and 29 percent of the students in those classes chose Account 1.)

12. I have exact counts for the students in my 1986 freshman course; the results are reported in "Teaching English for Reflective Thinking." At the beginning of fall 1986, 50 percent of the students mentioned trustworthiness of sources when justifying their choice one of the accounts.

13. At the beginning of fall 1986, 29 percent of the students justified their choice of an account on the basis of its consistency with things they knew about the war.

14. In the study reported in "Teaching English as Reflective Thinking," one of the categories of reasons for choosing an account is "plausibility and quality of claims and facts." At the beginning of fall 1986, 65 percent of the students mentioned reasons that were judged to fit that category. In my discussion here, however, I have separated "factuality" and "plausibility," criteria that were conflated in the earlier study.

15. Although I tinkered with the readings I used for this assignment over the years, the following sources constituted the core for the project (listed here in the order in which I assigned them).

READING ASSIGNMENT 1: THE TWO VIEWS

Stephen T. Hosmer, *Viet Cong Repression and Its Implications for the Future* (Lexington, MA: Heath, 1970), 46–51.

Noam Chomsky and Edward S. Herman, *Counter-Revolutionary Violence: Bloodbaths in Myth and Propaganda* Module 57 (Andover, MA: Warner Module Publications, 1973), 27–29.

READING ASSIGNMENT 2: THE "MASSACRE" VIEW

"The Massacre of Hué," *Time*, 31 Oct. 1969, 32–33.

Stewart Harris, "An Efficient Slaughter," *Time*, 5 April 1968, 36.

Don Oberdorfer, *Tet! The Turning Point in the Vietnam War* (New York: Da Capo Press, 1971), 199–202, 210–16, 221–35.

Alje Vennema, *The Vietcong Massacre at Hué* (New York: Vantage Press, 1976), excerpts from 96, 97, 98, 99, 116, 117–118, 119, 120, 121–22, 128–29, 134–35, 137, 139–41, 184–85.

READING ASSIGNMENT 3: THE "MYTH" VIEW

D. Gareth Porter and Len E. Ackland, "Vietnam: The Bloodbath Argument," *The Christian Century*, 5 Nov. 1969, 1414–17.

Edward Herman and D. Gareth Porter, "The Myth of the Hué Massacre," *Ramparts*, May 1975, 8–10, 12–13.

D. Gareth Porter, "The 1968 'Hué Massacre,'" *Indochina Chronicle*, June 1974. Rpt. in *The Congressional Record—Senate*, 19 February 1975, 3515–19.

16. For bibliographic information on Chomsky and Herman and subsequently mentioned sources, see note 15. These books and articles are not included in the Works Cited.

17. In terms of which account they chose, the students' responses were about the same at the end of the course as they were at the beginning: in both cases, considerably more students chose the second account as more believable. At the beginning of fall 1986, 25 percent chose Account 1 and 44 percent chose Account 2, while at the end of the semester 20 percent chose 1 and 39 percent chose 2 (the rest could not decide on an account). At the beginning of fall 1989, 29 percent chose Account 1 and 48 percent chose Account 2, while at the end of the course 23 percent chose 1 and 49 percent chose 2.

18. At the beginning of the semester fifty-seven students made statements that were classified as "skeptical" about judging what happened at Ap Bac; of those, 33 percent were categorized as

"perspectivist," 56 percent as "intuitive," and 9 percent as "analytical." At the end of the semester, sixty-one students made "skeptical" statements, but the percentage of "perspectivist" responses declined dramatically, to only 13 percent, while the percentage of intuitive responses increased to 75 percent and analytical responses to 12 percent. See Kroll, "Teaching English for Reflective Thinking."

19. The trends toward higher-level orientations at the end of the course were modest, overshadowed by the fact that a great many students relied on what I termed intuitive (or "quasi-analytical") reasons for selecting a particular account, whether at the beginning or end of the course. As reported in "Teaching English for Reflective Thinking," when I assigned scores to students' responses on the basis of the rating they received for conceptual orientation, the mean postcourse score (3.12) was higher than the mean precourse score (2.94). Although the difference between mean scores was statistically significant, the difference was small and strength of the effect quite weak. Those weak results are consistent with a good deal of research on intellectual development in the college years: conceptual growth is slow, and students do not typically undergo radical transformations of their thinking in one course or a single semester of college work.

On the basis of further analysis and reflection, I now have reservations about treating students' responses to the Ap Bac problem as the sole index of their orientations to discrepant accounts. In my recent work, therefore, I have moved away from a quantitative approach to students' responses, relying more heavily on a case-analysis approach which considers the Ap Bac exercise as one document in a student's portfolio of materials, each piece of which may contribute insight into a student's struggle with epistemological complexity.

20. In my emphasis on practice and application, I was following Dewey's principles for teaching reflective thinking. As Deanna Kuhn has succinctly summarized this view: "the only effective way to teach people to think is to engage them in thinking"

(502). Thus my pedagogy was based on what Moffett, in his essay "Learning to Write by Writing," calls an "action-response model"—a model whose central tenet is simply that people learn "by doing and by heeding what happens" (46). I tried to design my course so that students would have multiple opportunities to do reflective inquiry and to heed the results. And I tried to respond to students' efforts in ways that would be both supportive and challenging—supporting students when they engaged in comparative and evaluative thinking, challenging them to become more critical and reflective in their deliberations.

5. Ethical Inquiry

1. My use of a "moral dilemma" invites comparison with Lawrence Kohlberg's well-known and widely respected research on moral development (for example, *The Psychology of Moral Development*). Like Kohlberg, I was interested in examining people's ethical reasoning, and I found dilemmas to be a fruitful way to elicit their thoughts on moral problems, as well as a good way to stimulate the kind of discussion and reflection that leads to growth in moral reasoning. I learned a lot from examining Kohlberg's dilemmas and practicing his methods for analyzing people's responses to them. (In 1985, I spent a week at Harvard's Center for Moral Education, participating in a "moral judgment scoring workshop" conducted by Kohlberg and his colleagues.) But for this project, I did not adopt some of Kohlberg's theoretical assumptions (such as those concerning stage and sequence), and I did not use his scoring methods to analyze students' responses to the Rifleman's Dilemma. My project was closer in aim and method to Bardige's study of adolescents' responses to the Holocaust, although I learned about her work at the end of my project.

2. The Rifleman's Dilemma is a variant of a widely discussed situation that soldiers face in combat. In *Just and Unjust Wars*, Michael Walzer notes that the "same tale appears again and again in war memoirs and in letters from the front. It has this general

form: a soldier on patrol or on sniper duty catches an enemy soldier unaware, holds him in his gunsight, easy to kill, and then must decide whether to shoot him or let the opportunity pass" (138–39).

3. In fall 1986, 110 students completed the dilemma (at both the beginning and end of the course) and also gave me permission to use their responses; in fall 1989, the number was 91. At the beginning of the course, the percentage of students who said to shoot the woman was 73 percent in fall 1986 and 76 percent in fall 1989. In both 1986 and 1989, 20 percent of the students said that the rifleman should hold his fire. The rest proposed an alternative course of action.

4. The problem stated that "the squad was too far away for Johnson to call out to them. Even a warning shot would probably not stop them from proceeding around the bend." Nevertheless, several students felt that a warning shot was the most appropriate action, since it *might* give the squad time to prepare for whatever danger lay ahead. Faced with a choice between shooting the woman or holding fire, some students said Johnson should do neither.

In my opinion he should do neither. I think he should put his rifle on semiautomatic and shoot a round to the woman's side and observe her actions. This answer is the best solution that I can think of because: it gives Private Johnson a chance to see what the woman will do, it gives him time to act if the woman is still intent on his squad, and if she runs away, no one would have to be killed. [M/FR/S86]

Another approach was to suggest that Johnson should shoot to wound or disable, rather than kill, the woman.

Shoot, but not to kill. . . . If he shoots in order to wing her, he can keep his squad safe and possibly keep the woman alive if she is innocent. [F/FR/F86]

At the beginning of fall 1986, 7 percent of the students specified

189

an alternative course of action; in fall 1989, 4 percent suggested an alternative solution.

5. In fall 1986, 47 percent of the freshmen tried to figure the odds; in 1989, 41 percent did so.

6. One point of contention, particularly at the beginning of the semester, was whether women should be considered part of the guerrilla forces. Some students believed that women were not usually engaged in such activities.

> I really don't believe that women were sent to set off mines and booby traps. I think it was left up to the men. Chances are she is very frightened of the American soldiers and she has just spotted [them] and is trying to hide from them. [F/FR/F86]

Others said that the VC employed women as saboteurs.

> Johnson should understand that the VC used guerrilla tactics often to kill the enemy. The VC would recruit women and children to set traps, bombs, etc. [M/FR/F86]

7. In fall 1986, 45 percent of the students attempted to assess the consequences of the two choices; in fall 1989, 52 percent of the students used this strategy.

8. Nearly half of the students (48 percent) took this approach in fall 1986. However, in fall 1989, only 35 percent did so.

9. Not many students mentioned Johnson's relationship with his comrades as a reason for shooting: only 12 percent in fall 1986, 11 percent in fall 1989.

10. The story appears in Baker 209–12.

11. For an account of what happened at My Lai, see Hersh. One of my freshmen was struck by the fact that she was born on the day when the massacre occurred. During an interview she said the following: "I was born when it was going on. . . . Really freaked me out for like a month. I just—like the thought of me being born at the same time all these people—and so I've been affected by that. God, you know, life and death. It's really weird" [F/FR/F86].

12. In 1986, 14 percent of the students changed their decision from "don't shoot" to "shoot"; in 1989, 15 percent did so.

13. In 1986, 5 percent of the students changed their decision from "don't shoot" to "shoot," while in 1989, only 3 percent did so.

14. The percentages were as follows: in fall 1986, 73 percent of the students said to shoot at the beginning of the semester, while 82 percent did so at the end; in fall 1989, 76 percent said to shoot at the beginning and 89 percent made that decision at the end. Thus, after taking the course, more students decided that the rifleman should shoot the woman.

15. The percentages of students who mentioned calculating the consequences were as follows: in fall 1986, 45 percent (beginning) and 49 percent (end); in fall 1989, 52 percent (beginning) and 51 percent (end).

16. The percentages of students who mentioned "doing one's duty" were as follows: in fall 1986, 48 percent (beginning) and 35 percent (end); in fall 1989, 35 percent (beginning) and 25 percent (end).

17. In 1986, the percentage of students who weighed the odds increased only slightly, from 47 percent (beginning) to 51 percent (end). However, in 1989, the percentages increased from 41 percent (beginning) to 60 percent (end).

6. Lessons

1. Although some students complained about the amount of reading and writing they were asked to do and others were unhappy with a particular book or assignment, overall students were remarkably enthusiastic about the course. Below are four examples, one from each of the classes I taught, of the kinds of comments I found in the course evaluations that I collected at the end of the semester.

This is the best course I have had in eleven semesters as an undergraduate. . . . an excellent course, but not an easy one. I've never put in more time outside the class for any other course. It's been very time-consuming, but worth it. I've learned a lot about the Vietnam War, a lot about writing, a lot about different forms of literature, and a lot about ideas of morality, reality, and sanity. (Spring 1986)

I learned a lot. Not only on the war and English, but on life. It showed me how to read through BS and come to my own conclusions. It brought me to other cultures. . . . I learned about myself, what I believed in and why. (Fall 1986)

The course was the best I've taken at Indiana University. Through the readings and class discussion, I came to new awareness about myself, the war, and the world in which we live. I was continually challenged to rethink opinions and beliefs I had formulated out of ignorance. I not only learned about the war itself, but also about the people who fought, myself, and what it means to be human. (Spring 1988)

This course has had a tremendous effect on me. It is a very intense course with a great deal of reading and writing, but I feel it was all worth it. The course caused me to do a lot of self-exploration, and through this I became a better critical thinker and had more analytic ability. (Fall 1989)

2. This "open-ended" format was similar to the procedure that Perry used in his studies; see *Intellectual and Ethical Development*. I tape-recorded the interviews and later transcribed relevant portions.

3. In mid-January 1991, Ann wrote to tell me about her response to the Gulf War, an event that caused her to reflect on the Vietnam class she had taken as a freshman:

As times get worse, I think of your class. You would be the one person I'd like to talk to today. Sometimes . . . I think if only Congress had [had] a slide show with the projection of war on the screen, maybe the vote would have gone differently. I wish it had.

Works Cited

Baker, Mark. *Nam: The Vietnam War in the Words of the Men and Women Who Fought There.* New York: Quill, 1982.

Bardige, Betty. "Things So Finely Human: Moral Sensibilities at Risk in Adolescence." In *Mapping the Moral Domain,* edited by Carol Gilligan, Janie Victoria Ward, and Jill McLean Taylor. Cambridge: Harvard UP, 1988.

Belenky, Mary Field, Blythe McVicker Clinchy, Nancy Rule Goldberger, and Jill Mattuck Tarule. *Women's Ways of Knowing: The Development of Self, Voice, and Mind.* New York: Basic Books, 1986.

Booth, Wayne C. *The Company We Keep: An Ethics of Fiction.* Berkeley: U California P, 1988.

Broyles, William, Jr. "Why Men Love War." *Esquire,* Nov. 1984, 55–65.

Christie, N. Bradley. "Teaching Our Longest War: Constructive Lessons from Vietnam." *English Journal,* April 1989, 35–38.

"The Classroom Vietnam War." *Newsweek,* 11 March 1985, 75–76.

Clifford, John, ed. *The Experience of Reading: Louise Rosenblatt and Reader-Response Theory.* Portsmouth, NH: Boynton/Cook, 1991.

Dewey, John. *How We Think.* 1933. The Later Works, Vol. 8. Carbondale: Southern Illinois UP, 1986.

Ehrhart, W. D. "Teaching the Vietnam War." *Joiner Center Newsletter,* July 1990, 1–3.

Enders, William Bliss. "Teaching Vietnam: Reflections Beyond the Immediate." *English Journal,* December 1984, 28–30.

Works Cited

Farrell, Edmund J., and James R. Squire, eds. *Transactions with Literature: A Fifty-Year Perspective*. Urbana, IL: NCTE, 1990.

Franklin, Karen. "Vietnam 101: The Lessons of the War Have Reached America's Classrooms." *Veteran*, June 1988, 20–22.

Giroux, Henry A. *Theory and Resistance in Education*. South Hadley, MA: Bergin & Garvey, 1983.

Hayslip, Le Ly. *When Heaven and Earth Changed Places*. New York: Doubleday, 1989.

Hellman, John. *Fables of Fact*. Urbana: U of Illinois P, 1981.

Hersh, Seymour M. *My Lai 4: A Report on the Massacre and Its Aftermath*. New York: Random House, 1970.

Kirkpatrick, Charles E. "Bernard Fall Lived the Protracted War He Wrote About So Vividly and Knowledgeably." *Vietnam*, Winter 1988, 8, 78, 80, 82.

———. "Decision in the Northern Delta." *Vietnam*, June 1990, 47–53.

Kitchener, Karen. "Educational Goals and Reflective Thinking." *The Educational Forum* 48 (1983): 75–95.

———. "The Reflective Judgment Model: Characteristics, Evidence, and Measurement." In *Adult Cognitive Development: Methods and Models*, edited by R. A. Mines and K. S. Kitchener. New York: Praeger, 1986.

Kitchener, Karen S., and Patricia M. King. "Reflective Judgment: Concepts of Justification and Their Relationship to Age and Education." *Journal of Applied Developmental Psychology* 2 (1981): 89–116.

———. "The Reflective Judgment Model: Transforming Assumptions About Knowing." In *Fostering Critical Reflection in Adulthood*, edited by Jack Mezirow. San Francisco: Jossey-Bass, 1990.

Kohlberg, Lawrence. *The Psychology of Moral Development*. San Francisco: Harper and Row, 1984.

Kroll, Barry M. "Observing Students' Reflective Thinking: A Teacher-Research Project." In *The Writing Teacher as Researcher: Essays in the Theory and Practice of Class-Based Research*, edited by Donald A. Daiker and Max Morenberg. Portsmouth, NH: Heinemann, 1990.

———. "Teaching English for Reflective Thinking." In *Developing Discourse Practices in Adolescence and Adulthood*, edited by Richard Beach and Susan Hynds. Norwood, NJ: Ablex, 1990.

Kuhn, Deanna. "Education for Thinking." *Teachers College Record* 87 (1986): 495–512.

Maclear, Michael. *The Ten Thousand Day War, Vietnam: 1945–1975*. New York: Avon, 1981.

Moffett, James. *Teaching the Universe of Discourse*. Boston: Houghton Mifflin, 1968.

Newman, John. *Vietnam War Literature: An Annotated Bibliography of Imaginative Works About Americans Fighting in Vietnam*. 2nd ed. Metuchen, NJ: Scarecrow Press, 1988.

Ngoc, Nguyen. *The Will of Heaven*. New York: Dutton, 1982.

Nussbaum, Martha C. *Love's Knowledge: Essays on Philosophy and Literature*. New York: Oxford UP, 1990.

Olham, Perry. "On Teaching Vietnam War Literature." *English Journal*, Feb. 1986, 55–56.

Paul, Richard. *Critical Thinking*. Rohnert Park, CA: Center for Critical Thinking and Moral Critique, 1990.

———. "Critical Thinking: Fundamental to Education for a Free Society." *Educational Leadership*, Sept. 1984, 4–14.

Perry, William G., Jr. "Cognitive and Ethical Growth: The Making of Meaning." In *The Modern American College*, edited by Arthur Chickering. San Francisco: Jossey-Bass, 1981.

———. *Forms of Intellectual and Ethical Development in the College Years*. New York: Holt, Rinehart and Winston, 1970.

Rosenblatt, Louise M. *Literature as Exploration*. Rev. ed. New York: Noble and Noble, 1968.

———. *The Reader, the Text, the Poem*. Carbondale: Southern Illinois UP, 1978.

Sheehan, Neil. *A Bright Shining Lie: John Paul Vann and America in Vietnam*. New York: Random House, 1988.

Works Cited

Shor, Ira. *Critical Thinking and Everyday Life*. Chicago: U of Chicago P, 1987.

Siegel, Harvey. *Educating Reason: Rationality, Critical Thinking, and Education*. New York: Routledge, 1988.

Stanton, Shelby. *The Rise and Fall of an American Army: U.S. Ground Forces in Vietnam, 1965–1973*. Novato, CA: Presidio, 1985.

Starr, Jerold M. *The Lessons of the Vietnam War*. Pittsburgh: Center for Social Studies Education, 1988.

————. "The Making of *The Lessons of the Vietnam War*." *Social Education*, Jan. 1988, 29–32.

Summers, Harry G. *Vietnam War Almanac*. New York: Facts on File, 1985.

Walzer, Michael. *Just and Unjust Wars*. New York: Basic Books, 1977.

Wittman, Sandra M. *Writing About Vietnam: A Bibliography of the Vietnam Conflict*. Boston: G. K. Hall, 1989.

Zimbardo, Philip G. *Psychology and Life*. 11th ed. Glenview, IL: Scott, Foresman, 1985.

Index

Index

Index

Journals: assignment, 8–9; comments in margins, 97–98, 101, 129; criteria for grading, 178n.7; excerpts, identifying students, ix–x; excerpts, selecting, 178n.8; personal expression, 13, 22, 41; response log, 11; review ideas, 12; senior interviews, 158–59; value for difficult texts, 55, 71

Karen: affected by course, 151; Ap Bac response, 107–8, 111–12; connected inquiry, 21–22; on *Dispatches*, 59–61; ethical inquiry, 143–49; Hué unit, 108–11; introduction to, 9; on poetry, 62–63; on Rifleman's Dilemma, 144–45; talk with father, 35–37, 180–81n.7
Killing, morality of. *See* Ethical inquiry
Killing, personal response, 22, 37–41
Kohlberg, Lawrence, 188n.1
Komunyaka, Yusef. *See Dien Cai Dau*
Kovic, Ron. *See Born on the Fourth of July*

Literary inquiry, 45, 153–54. *See also* Literary judgment; Poetry
Literary judgment: change of criteria, 61, 64, 72; criteria, general, 46–47; criterion of artistry, 47, 52–53, 57–59, 61–63, 65, 69; criterion of authenticity, 47, 49–51, 59–61, 71–72; criterion of intensity, 47–49, 56–57

Literature as Exploration. See Rosenblatt, Louise M.
Logbook. *See* Journals

Men, responses to personal narratives, 24, 26. *See also* Edward
Moral dilemmas: in *Fields of Fire*, 138–41, 149–50; reveal teacher's judgments, 131–32; in *A Rumor of War*, 127–31, 145–46, 149–50. *See also* Ethical inquiry; Rifleman's Dilemma
Murder of civilians, 113–14, 133, 147. *See also* Ethical inquiry; Moral dilemmas; My Lai Massacre
My Lai Massacre, 136–38, 147–48

O'Brien, Tim. *See Going After Cacciato*
Oral histories. *See* Critical stance; *Everything We Had*

Painting, expression through, 41–42
Perry Scheme, 82–83, 87, 183n.5, 192n.2
Personal narratives. *See Everything We Had; Home Before Morning; Rumor of War, A*
Poetry, negative attitude, 62–63
Pragmatist orientation, 10, 178n.11. *See also* Dewey, John
Principled morality, 139–40

Questions: asking, 72; feelings into reflections, 42

Reflective Judgment Model, 82–83, 183–84n.6

Index

Barry M. Kroll is an associate professor of English at Indiana University, Bloomington, where he directs the writing program and teaches courses in composition and literature. He served as an Army officer in Vietnam during 1969 and 1970.